How to Sail the Atlantic Alone

How to Sail the Atlantic Alone

Ed and Fran Lormand

David McKay Company, Inc.
NEW YORK

Library of Congress Cataloging in Publication Data

Lormand, Ed.
How to sail the Atlantic alone.

Bibliography: p.
1. Lormand, Ed. 2. Voyages and travels—
1951-   3. Atlantic Ocean. 4. Travelers—
United States—Biography. I. Lormand, Fran,
joint author. II. Title.
G470.L63   910'.09'1631   79-25001
ISBN 0-679-51082-6

10 9 8 7 6 5 4 3 2 1

We lovingly dedicate this book to each other. Without us it never would have been possible.

Why?

Its sensuous beauty
and the manner it parties
with stars and sun and cloud,
in subtlety and boldness,
in darkness and light,
the sea pulls to me.
I can measure my mental,
emotional and physical status
by the ocean strength,
and I surge with joy
at the growth in me
by association.
And I know
that the oceans of the world
wash carelessly,
without motive
good or evil
on the shores of continents and
islands all over this ball,
and I know
that the oceans churn and nurture
the mightiest and meekest
of earth's animals and plants,
and I know
that the oceans are likely
the original womb of all life here,
and with all this,
the oceans seem timeless but are not.
And I, nonetheless, am satisfied
with their nearness to immortality.

Beau Cutts

CONTENTS

PART 1

*Preparing for
the Voyage*

1

Fantasy to Fact

One of the first major hurdles in an independent adventure is overcoming disbelief. And one must not ridicule the scoffers. Their attitude, in our case anyway, was entirely reasonable. Their old friend, the 138-pound music teacher, had been talking for years about crossing oceans aboard his sailboat. He had started talking about it long before he owned a sailboat, in the days when we made two or three trips a day to the docks to "look at the boats." For years we had been card-carrying members of the local wharf rat community, inspecting every transient sailboat that stopped, talking to the crews, and accepting instantly any invitation to go sailing. We learned something new every time, and our preparation was conscious, deliberate, and more or less patient. Witnesses to our single-minded determination over the years should not have been surprised when our plans solidified, but apparently no one had been paying attention.

Then all of a sudden the word became flesh. The dream turned into reality on a beautiful weekend early in the spring of 1975. Ed and I, along with a mixed group of family and friends, were weekending at my mother's house, Sea Sand, at Fernandina Beach, Florida. From my place at the dinner table I had an unobstructed view of low white dunes anchored by golden sea oats bending in the breeze, and beyond that the Atlantic Ocean tumbling gently onto the wide sandy beach.

"I am going to sail *Folly* from here to Plymouth, England," Ed announced, "to celebrate the Bicentennial."

"Pass the chicken," somebody commanded.

"I will leave," Ed continued, "on June 10, 1976, at 10:00 A.M." One or two forks paused, and someone said. "When?"

That instant marked the end of the daydream and the beginning of the physical labor.

And if you are a 138-pound schoolteacher (or a 238-pound accountant) and you have always wanted to sail the Atlantic alone on your own boat, you can—if you really want to—because we did it.

If the first part of the project is to convince people that you are really going, the second part is to convince some other people that you are coming back. The first group is made up of the friends, relatives, fellow workers, other sailing nuts, and chance acquaintances who have been listening for the past seven years to your announcement that you will sail the Atlantic alone on your own boat. The second group is made up of your bank, insurance company (any insurance company), and your mother.

In our case, during the first few of the seven years the skepticism of the first group was reasonable, and the anxiety of the second group was dormant. At that time we owned an eleven-and-a-half-foot sailboat that we had built ourselves and that we had, in a moment of brilliant foresight, named *Tippecanoe*. Now, after a couple of quantum jumps, we were the astonished possessors (along with the aforementioned bank) of a Yankee 28 sloop.

Naming a date and time shifted perspectives and attitudes—ours as well as everybody else's. To set a departure date the day after Ed's last official day of work at school, with *Folly* 325 miles away from our Atlanta apartment, might have sounded naive to those of our friends who truly grasped the gravity of the situation, but as I look back, I'm not sure anyone except the two of us really comprehended it.

We certainly knew better. We had read every book on ocean sailing, both singlehanded and crewed, we could find. We culled every bit of information we could from accounts of the voyages of Columbus, Magellan, the Spanish Armada, the Polynesians, Joshua Slocum, the Smeetons, the Hiscocks, the Roths, Chichester, and on through the shelves of the Atlanta Public Library. We bought our own copies when we could find them and afford them. We read all the boat magazines from cover to cover. Our bookshelves sagged. Towering stacks of magazines dominated our apartment's decor, along with mountains of brochures on every piece of equipment that could conceivably be used on a twenty-eight-foot sailboat.

We talked to sailors. We learned what to expect and what to do, and often we learned by graphic example what *not* to do.

You must do the research. You must know what is involved.

In every account of a singlehanded small-boat voyage that we had read, the captain had quit his shore-side job at least a month before departure time to devote himself full-time to the boat and last-minute preparations. I had a feeling there was a good reason for that. I was right.

But 10:00 A.M., June 10, 1976, remained a constant. After years of studying the pilot atlases, charts, coast pilots, and sailing directions, Ed would have preferred to leave Fernandina Beach in May, but the administrators of DeKalb College, where he taught, were unlikely to change the school calendar for something so frivolous and self-indulgent as a singlehanded transatlantic voyage—Bicentennial or no. Sometimes it is necessary to accommodate oneself to the realities. And so to work.

With heroic determination you have made up your mind and set the date. The next step involves—face it—money. You are going to do this yourself, remember? Being a schoolteacher helps in that summer work is extra, and more important, it's optional. But if you are not a teacher, concentrate. You'll think of something.

Ed arranged to teach a full load in the college's 1975 summer session. Staying in Atlanta for the summer instead of going to Florida also meant that Ed could continue to teach a few private students at home. More money. It also meant we would have to buy more gasoline to support our habit. We didn't have the self-discipline to stay away from *Folly* on summer weekends. We had congratulated ourselves on our energy-consciousness when we bought a sailboat, and we derided the stinkpots as they roared past us on the water. Then we roared up and down the highway aboard Samuel A. Maverick 650 miles every weekend. So much for responsible citizenship.

But money was primary. How could a college music teacher have the temerity even to dream of a transatlantic voyage on his own boat? Well, if other people could do it, so could we. We believed firmly that if a dream was important enough to us, we could make it come true. We had had some prior successful experience with that theory.

Unless you are independently wealthy (in which case you can stop reading now, anyway), you need an administrative assistant who will work for nothing more than room and board and fringe benefits (something like a wife or husband). We toyed with the idea of my getting a job and quickly discarded it. If Ed were to work every waking moment at teaching, and if he really wanted to leave on June 10, I would have to do the organization work— gathering information, taking care of correspondence, running errands to order and pick up new equipment, and making sure we observed mealtimes and wore relatively clean clothes. We couldn't both work outside. Ed would have to make the money, and I would do the leg and paper work. It turned out to be a very interesting job.

First you have to make a list. And first on the list is the boat.

There we were lucky. *Lormand's 2nd Folly* (successor to the *1st*—a Windjammer 17) is a Yankee 28, a fiberglass sloop designed by Robert Finch of Sparkman & Stephens. She was designed as a racer-cruiser in the half-ton category according to 1972-vintage rules. In June 1974, when we bought her, she had hardly been sailed at all. She had spent one year as a Jackson-ville, Florida, dealer's demonstrator, and a few months after he sold her, the new owner was transferred away from Jacksonville. The wedges had never been put on the mast. In fact, the only evidence of use was an unopened can of root beer in the icebox.

We have always been primarily interested in cruising, not rac-ing. We subscribe to the theory that where two sailboats under-way are gathered together, a race exists. In that sense we are competitive, but we had never been lured by more formal rac-ing. We had no objection to the fact that *Folly* sailed beautifully, was respectably swift, and had a clean, comfortable deck. But it was also important to us that she was spacious and comfortable enough below for extended living aboard. In terms of our long-range plans the quality of her rigging and deck fittings—much heavier than usually found in an American-built stock boat—took on real financial significance. I won't say that the *2nd Folly* was more than we expected in our wildest dreams; we've been known to have some fairly wild dreams. (So have you, I trust.) But she was certainly more than we expected in our more lucid moments.

Ed had wanted a boat we could take offshore at least for short sails in good weather. I had wanted a boat with a galley and a head. What we got was a boat with a galley and a head that could go almost anywhere.

That is not to say she was ready to stock with food and water and set sail. Going to sea would be more complicated than that. But she did not need any real structural modifications or strengthening. That fact fueled our dreaming.

In June 1975, a year before departure, Ed made a list of equipment he would need and projects to complete. It was a long list, and the items were marked according to priority.

In an activity like singlehanded ocean voyaging, mountain climbing, or sky or scuba diving, you have only one decision to make and that is whether or not you are going to do it. Once you have decided to do it, you are committed—body, mind, soul, and pocketbook. There can be no carelessness and very little com-promising. The only question to ask at each step along the way is, "What is the best piece of equipment I can get to fulfill this particular function on a boat this size on a voyage of this nature?" The object, after all, is survival.

Ed pondered his equipment list. He pored over articles in boat magazines and dog-eared the pages so that I could go through them later and send off for brochures on things that interested him. He took each item, researched it, and made a decision. In the margins of his notebook he estimated costs.

At the same time I began another kind of intelligence-gathering. I called the British Consulate in Atlanta and asked for information about Plymouth. That's where the Pilgrims had sailed from. Ed was going in 1976 in his own private Bicentennial celebration. That took care of that decision. He would sail from Fernandina Beach to Plymouth, England.

I wanted the names of yacht clubs and/or marinas, I said to the cool British voice, because my husband was going to sail our twenty-eight-foot sloop to Plymouth next summer. The voice replied that she would send me whatever she could find, including the address of the Chamber of Commerce. In my log dated June 24, I wrote, "Sounded as if she got a request like that every day." We later found her response to be typically British. Americans were horrified.

But don't be discouraged.

The British attitude was, "Doesn't everyone?" At any rate, a packet of British maps, tourist and customs information, and the address of the Plymouth Chamber of Commerce appeared in our next day's mail. I wrote the Chamber of Commerce and asked about yacht clubs and marinas.

Also in my June 24 log entry, I indicated that we had begun our early efforts to find an insurance company willing to cover *Folly*. Later we were very happy that we had started looking a year in advance. And by now I had begun researching types of emergency foods, camping foods, and lists of food supplies carried by other singlehanders.

During the year since we had bought *Folly*, we had added

several major pieces of equipment. The Hood 150 percent genoa originally cut for *Folly* surfaced at a boat equipment store we frequented. *Folly*'s original sails had been dispersed throughout the Jacksonville area after a slight misunderstanding between the original dealer and the first owner. The owner had subsequently bought a Johnson mainsail and working jib, and that was *Folly*'s sail inventory when we bought her. We made an offer. It was refused. We waited several months and made the same offer. It was accepted, and we had a beautiful 150 percent genny.

We had also bought a Ritchie SN-B-45 compass, a Gladding Gulfstream RDF, and two safety harnesses. To *Folly*'s Danforth 13-S anchor we had added a #40 Viking storm anchor. And among our very first purchases were a gimbaled Optimus two-burner alcohol stove and four type-1 lifejackets legal for off-shore use—bulky, uncomfortable, and reliable. That was our head start.

By August 1975, we had planned almost everything else we wanted to add for Ed's trip, from building the self-steering gear (we had the plans) to netting in the cabin shelves and securing the storage lockers below. Our list of equipment was organized; and with summer-session cash in hand, we took it to Vic Lipscomb at Whitehead Sailboat Company (now Lipscomb Sailboat Company) in Atlanta.

We ordered:

> A new tiller (the old one would be a spare)
> Lower lifelines (we had the uppers, and the stanchions were already fitted for lowers, and we're cowards)
> Kerosene running lights (large ones)
> Mast bail
> 6 spare blocks (two of them snatch blocks)
> A 600-foot spool of half-inch nylon twist line
> A 14-foot spinnaker pole (to be used as a whisker pole or a spare mast in case of dismasting)
> Engine spares for our Atomic 4
> Spare stainless steel snap shackle
> 2 #40 Lewmar winches (our #16's wouldn't provide

enough muscle for a singlehander, and with the
40's Fran could handle the genoa alone, which was
reason enough to get them)

We placed that order on August 5, 1975. The last item on this
list to arrive was the kerosene stern light. It arrived on June 3,
1976, one week before Ed's departure. We suspected the company of sculpting one by hand just for us. But by Labor Day,
1975, we had installed the sheet winches, the mast bail, and the
tiller (which we had hung on a coat hanger in our guest room
closet and varnished and fitted ourselves), and we had aboard
four of the spare blocks, the snap shackle, the half-inch line, and
assorted stainless steel nuts, bolts, screws, and washers. And the
spinnaker pole was in Sea Sand's garage. *Folly* was changing
visibly. We had spent about $1,000. Scoffers were turning into
believers.

You will want the support and encouragement of your family,
especially, and your friends, but you can't spend a lot of time
trying to convince people. You will be too busy.

My mother was closer to the preparations than anyone else.
She was with us when we bought the *2nd Folly,* and we saw her
on almost all of our trips south either at her home in Waycross,
Georgia, or in Fernandina. She had been listening to our tall
tales for years, along with everybody else, but she was probably
the first to realize that with a date set, the fantasy had materi-
alized.

Ed's family presented something of a problem. They were in
Louisiana, and while Ed's father knew about the trip, his mother
did not. When other Louisiana friends came to the beach for a
visit early in the summer, they brought a message from Papa
Lormand. "Do not, under any circumstances, tell your mother."
And the Lormands were coming to see us on their vacation in
August.

My immediate reaction was that they should stay away. All of
our friends and relatives in Georgia and Florida knew more

about our plans than they really wanted to. I didn't see how Mama Lormand could be with us for two weeks and not pick up a hint. But she was, and she didn't, although there were a couple of close calls.

Her being totally unaware of what Ed was going to do placed something of a strain on him. He wanted her to understand what he was doing and why, and he wanted her to be included in his plans and to be fully informed about his preparations. But we followed his father's orders.

My mother, on the other hand, began to think of our antics as the world's greatest spectator sport. She asked questions. She examined each new piece of equipment as it appeared. She watched us take our plastic sextant (which she had given us) out on the beach to practice shooting and then saw us sitting at the table for hours working out the sights. She was sometimes exasperated by our one-track minds and unpredictable arrivals and departures, but we had her support—especially when other people expressed doubts about our sanity.

"The reason so many people think it's such a horrible thing to do," she said to me early in the year, "is that they just don't know anything about it."

At one point in our preparations she even confessed that she could imagine wanting to do something like that herself. And she read accounts of other singlehanders. After reading Knox-Johnston, *Dove,* Milnes-Walker, Hiscock, and Roth, she could tell us how to solve most problems at sea, and she could compare our preparations with others'. She concluded that no one else had been more careful and that many had been foolhardy. It was at that point that one of her friends asked, "Aren't you terribly frightened about Ed's crossing the ocean in a sailboat?"

"No," she replied. "I'm a lot more frightened about crossing the ocean in an airplane when we go to meet him."

The attitudes of non-family were less important, but they did make a difference in the ease with which we could work. On August 20, 1975, I wrote in my log: "One by one our friends and relatives have stopped saying 'You're crazy' and have begun to asked interested questions. It's a relief to Ed to be taken seriously and not to have to fight psychological battles with nonbelievers every time the subject comes up." (Which will be all the time. Your friends are hungry for something to talk about besides work, politics, and soap operas.)

We were also amused by friends who couldn't seem to decide whether we were interesting now or just plain weird. Socially, should they invite us to join them alone, or were we presentable enough to include on their larger guest lists of normal people?

Actually their quandary was irrelevant. As the months went by, Ed was working every waking moment during the four and a half days that we were in Atlanta, and our weekend socializing in Fernandina included only those people who were working with us on boat projects and whoever happened to be visiting my mother at Sea Sand. Our social life dwindled and disappeared, and Sam's mileage rolled up.

After the expenditure of large sums of green cash had convinced everyone that Ed seriously intended to cast off *Folly*'s docklines on June 10, 1976, and sail to Plymouth, England, by himself, the next question was, "Why?" Everybody asked it. Almost everybody wanted an answer in twenty-five words or less. Those answers came easily. "Because it's 1976, the Bicentennial, and my boat is red, white, and blue. Because I turned forty in April."

"Because I want to go to England," I chimed in.

"I want to see Stonehenge," Ed often added. "I want to touch something that old."

But some questioners looked Ed squarely in the eye and challenged him for the truth, and that was more difficult. Many of them wanted real answers because they harbored similar dreams themselves. They were comparing notes, and it gave them hope to see someone bringing such a dream to life. Adventure, challenge, ultimate independence, passion for the sea and sailing.

"To test myself. To be my own doctor, lawyer, carpenter. Because I want to do it, and I think I can."

"Because he wants to." That was my basic answer. The reasons why he wanted to were so deeply a part of him and so complex that there was no answer. Often, in our research and preparation and also for pleasure, we read what other people had written about sailing, about adventure, and about their reasons. We shared them with each other, and Ed carried a few of them in his billfold. He would sometimes bring them out and try them on questioners to see if other sailors and adventurers had had any better luck at explaining themselves.

Joshua Slocum wrote, "You must then know the sea, and know that you know it, and not forget that it was made to be sailed over."

We liked that. In our own experience knowledge had bred confidence, and it was hard to have too much of either in a crisis situation. As for reasons why, "it was made to be sailed over" did seem to border on "because it is there."

Another quote appeared in *Summer of the Red Wolf*, a novel by Morris West. "There is no purer or more healing pleasure for a man than to stand helm watch in a fair wind and feel the buck of the sea and watch the white, tight belly of a well-set canvas." Sailors understood that.

Hemingway talked about solitary adventure. "If you serve time for society, democracy, and the other things quite young, and, declining any further enlistment make yourself responsible only to yourself, you exchange the pleasant, comforting stench of comrades for something you can never feel in any other way than by yourself." *(Green Hills of Africa).*

Why? You'll have to figure out your own reasons.

On Labor Day weekend, 1975, we went with the North Florida Cruising Club on our annual cruise to Cumberland Island. Ed's parents were visiting us at the beach, and Papa Lormand went on the cruise with Ed and me. We sailed *Folly* north behind Cumberland and anchored out from Greyfield dock. Separating us and the boat from Ed's mother for a few hours reduced slightly the risk of her finding out what we were up to. We also realized that this outing was likely to be our last strictly-for-pleasure overnight cruise and almost our last strictly-for-pleasure sail. From then on we could go sailing only to test new gear, although we freely confess that we might have gone sailing once or twice to test something like a new can opener.

As soon as our anchor was down, guests began rafting up.

Soon two friends, Jake Mottayaw and Bill Hogan, from Fernandina, were in the process of scheming a sea trial for Ed. They would go out to sea with him, let him do all the work—he wanted to singlehand so much—and see if he could pass their offshore test. Ed didn't need a lot of persuasion. It was another excuse to go sailing. Jake and Bill sailed back to Fernandina to continue plotting.

During the next week the men got their sea trial organized, and the three of them departed the Fernandina Beach city dock aboard *Folly* at 11:00 P.M. on Thursday night after Jake's City Commission budget meeting. (Jake was mayor of Fernandina.) It was the first time I had watched *Folly* sail away without me.

They had a beautiful trip. They sailed east forty or forty-five miles and had perfect weather except for six hours becalmed, during which time they played. Jake caught two king mackerel. He and Bill brought one aboard, cleaned it, and bloodied the boat, to the captain's horror. When they were forbidden to boat the second, they cut its head off, tied a line to its tail and attracted several hungry sharks to feed. They were then inspired to suggest that the would-be singlehander should practice a man-overboard drill. The captain, invoking the dictatorial powers of his position, refused.

They came back alive on Saturday, concluding thereby that Ed had passed the test.

2

Phase Two

Ed occasionally worried about the money we were spending on new equipment for a selfish project that would bring him pleasure. I assured him that he would not be singlehanding indefinitely and that I planned to reap my reward. I wanted all the new goodies for the cruising that we would do together. Since my own duties on deck usually involved the tiller or the jib sheet or both, while the captain did the heavy work on the foredeck or lay on a bunk below listening to the water go past the hull, I considered the new winches my own and wrote happily in my log, "I really can winch in the genny with my little finger—in a light breeze." We suspected that the hazard of the new winches lay in the possibility of pulling down the standing rigging when we used the lower gear.

We also installed a new kerosene lamp in the cabin over the galley. It helped in that dark corner, and now we could see into the icebox without a flashlight at night. The lamp was a little bit in the way of reaching into the icebox, but we would learn to get around it. We were learning that on a twenty-eight-foot sailboat, solving one problem often created another. For that reason we tried not to rush into installing any new piece of equipment until we had considered very carefully the pros and cons of all the possible locations and acknowledged whatever trade-offs we would be making in convenience. On our weekend trips to Fernandina we often spent hours just sitting in the cabin contemplating bulkhead and locker space, after which we had to try to think of an answer to "What were you *doing* all that time?" in a way that would justify our apparent inactivity. We had long since learned the futility of trying to explain to nonboating people the pure joy of simply sitting aboard one's own boat—an activity that for us, now, was a happy combination of business and pleasure.

Actually, beginning in September and continuing throughout the school year until the day of Ed's departure, constructive activity—either physical or mental—rarely slowed down. We had indulged our craving for the beach and sailing during the summer with trips to Fernandina every weekend. When the fall term began, we gave ourselves a firm lecture on economy, both financial and physical. There was work to do aboard *Folly*. There were also essential projects that could be finished entirely or partly away from the boat, and a 650-mile drive every weekend does begin to sap the energy after a while. We didn't want to be exhausted when we did get to the boat—not that early in the game anyway.

We wanted to put the old #16 winches behind the new ones, but Ed wanted to tear them down and clean and grease them before we put them back on the boat. Those could go to Atlanta with us.

The next project that he could now begin was to devise a way to get himself to the top of the mast. I had winched him up and down to get our wooden spreaders for refinishing, but now he needed a relatively secure way to get himself up alone. During some of his hours of meditating (the hours of driving up and down the highway were not wasted either), he had mentally designed a rope ladder that he could run up on a halyard, tying the two lower ends to the handrails on deck. He could split two-by-fours into two-by-twos for rungs, drill a hole in each end to run whatever length of our half-inch line was necessary to get him all the way up the mast, and with lighter line hold each rung in place.

Jake Mottayaw possessed skill amounting to artistry in wood-working. He also possessed a garage full of woodworking equipment, and with reckless abandon he offered us the use of his talent as well as his tools. Ed took the two-by-fours to Jake's to split them. We started work on the ladder in our garage at the beach and on Sunday packed up the project and took it to Atlanta to finish. We also took all the covers to the seat lockers so that Ed could work out a way to lock them down.

These projects were enough to keep us busy for several of our alternate stay-at-home weekends, and by the time we had finished them, we had other projects planned or underway. At one point, as June 10, 1976, drew near, my mother asked how in the world we had known what to do next at every step of the way so that we could get everything done on time. Simple, I told her. When we already had the necessary supplies and equipment to complete a project—or could get them easily—we went to work on that project without delay. In late September our half-inch line had arrived and we already had some treated two-by-fours in the garage, so we made the ladder.

Sometimes our next project was determined by what we could afford to buy next, or by the sudden appearance of someone who could get something we wanted for an unusually good price, or by the sheer blind luck of our appearing in the right place at the right instant.

Alec Jones, a former student of Ed's, was also a good friend and often our crew. He had a friend who sold emergency locator transmitters to airline companies. That meant we could get the kind of no-nonsense ELT an airliner carries for the same price as a smaller yacht-store version. We bought that quickly while the offer held.

The father of one of Ed's students worked for Panasonic and generously offered to help us find a sturdy tape recorder and tapes for Ed's daily tape log and a good radio with the frequencies for universal time checks.

And one day we went to Jacksonville to buy a new Walker taffrail log at a nautical supply store. We expected to write a check for $225 plus tax. First, however, we went out to Graham's Boat Yard to pick up a few other items. As we walked in the door at Graham's, Phil Thibodeau, the yard manager, looked up and said, "Come over here, Ed. This man has something you might be interested in."

It was a solid brass Walker log with a solid brass rotator. The line and weights were missing, but the log didn't need anything but polishing. Ed cradled the log in his hands and turned one end of the cylinder, opening one side of the log to show the three dials on its face.

"How much?" he asked.

"Seventy-five dollars," the man said. "I sail on the St. Johns River. Not much use for one of these."

Ed hedged. He shrugged, handing it back, said "I dunno," and walked around the store. Then he came back. "What if it doesn't work?"

"It works," the man said. "Well—I can't take less than sixty dollars."

"Write a check, baby," Ed commanded, reclaiming the log.

I wrote a check for $60 for a solid brass Walker log that was beautiful as well as functional—we hoped.

"If it doesn't work," Ed said as we left Graham's, "we can always hang it on the wall and admire it."

It worked. And it was like a blessing on our dreams.

Fall deepened into scarlet and gold beside the middle Georgia highways. The pecans ripened and fell with the leaves. Around the first of November we were in Fernandina when Malvina Finlayson arrived from England to visit her sister and brother-in-law, Phyllis and Dave Blacklock. Phyllis and Dave were our neighbors and good friends. She had grown up in Wells, Somerset, and he was a not-very-dour Scot. Both of them had taken a great interest in our plans, and Dave had generously given Ed a varied collection of stainless steel hardware and the use of any of his tools that might help us.

Now that we also knew Malvina, we had a real friend in England. She visited aboard *Folly* and at Sea Sand, and before she left Fernandina to return home, Ed suddenly decided to add one more to his list of reasons for going. He cut a dollar bill in half, gave one half to Malvina, and kept the other. Ed, a Louisiana Cajun, had often heard it said that a Cajun would do anything for a dollar. So he would sail the Atlantic to collect half of one.

Also in November it was time to have *Folly*'s bottom painted. It was fun taking her down the Intracoastal Waterway from Fernandina Beach to Graham's in Jacksonville—an excuse to go somewhere on the boat. The bottom would have to be painted again before June 10, but during the November haulout, we wanted to have everything done to the hull that we wanted the yard to do. Besides scraping barnacles and scrubbing and painting the bottom, we wanted anyone who worked on *Folly* to examine every part of her as if they were about to take off transatlantic themselves.

In our circumstances, having yard work done on *Folly* meant that we would pack Sam, leave Atlanta as early as possible on Friday afternoon and drive to Fernandina, arriving there around 9:00 P.M. if we were lucky. Next morning we would get up and get *Folly* out of her slip at Dell's Marina as early as the tide would allow and motor-sail the six- to seven-hour trip to Graham's. We would tidy up the boat, shift everything out of the way for the workmen, leave the key in the slot at the office, and ride back to Fernandina with whatever friend or relative had been persuaded to drive over to Jacksonville to pick us up. Sometimes we could get someone to drive a car to Graham's and leave it there beforehand. That meant driving two cars to Graham's to leave one there so that we could have transportation when we arrived. Then we could drive ourselves back to the beach. If this plan sounds complicated, it was.

We would arrive back in Fernandina for a late dinner Saturday night and drive back to Atlanta on Sunday. If the schedule sounds exhausting, it was that, too.

Graham's would have the boat to work on during the week and the next weekend we would organize our transportation and pick her up for the trip home. My mother took great pleasure in counting the number of cars it took to move one sailboat from one place to another. Sailboats, not to mention sailors, were a little silly anyway. I pointed out that if we just moved aboard *Folly* altogether, going only where she could take us, we wouldn't need cars at all. That was a very appealing prospect to me. No offense, Sam.

But the real beauty of our arrangement lay in our trust in Graham's Boat Yard. Their work for us had always been done properly and promptly, and we had no qualms about leaving *Folly* in their care to be worked on in our absence. On that November trip, in addition to the bottom-painting, on Ed's orders they checked the exhaust system for corrosion, installed new zincs on the shaft, replaced the engine intake strainer, and checked the propeller, shaft, packing gland, and through-hull drain. Then they installed two new 1½-inch cockpit scuppers. If a wave broke over *Folly*, filling the cockpit with water, the single drain we already had just didn't empty the cockpit fast enough to suit Ed.

There were two holes in the hull that Ed wanted closed—a fitting in the keel for a knotmeter (we didn't have one) and a hole that had been drilled at the factory for a head but had been covered thinly when a self-contained head was installed. Both of those holes were fiberglassed over on the outside.

The yard workers also measured the rudder while *Folly* was out of the water so that Ed could use these figures in his calculations for the self-steering gear.

We got *Folly* back to Fernandina again, and Thanksgiving gave us a long weekend. We took time out for cooking and eating Thanksgiving dinner and then went back to work, doing our best to explain our antisocial behavior.

We worked and drove and chipped away at our lists, which perversely were getting longer instead of shorter. Finally Ed's month-long Christmas vacation began. We had hoped for and halfway planned a trip down the Intracoastal Waterway during the first week or two of our vacation, but as the time approached, we faced the fact that we had been living in a dream world. We went to Fernandina and stayed there and worked.

One of the top-priority projects on our first list was the self-steering gear. Ed had studied self-steering devices since our *Tippecanoe* days. On *Lormand's 1st Folly*, the Windjammer 17, he had actually installed one on our cruise down the Waterway to Cape Canaveral. It had consisted of a piece of elastic and a piece of string and had worked for remarkably long periods as long as we sat still in the cockpit.

Among the various types of self-steering in use on cruising sailboats, one in particular had impressed him. He liked the principle behind it because it would give him a spare rudder in case of disaster to *Folly*'s own. The plans and specifications had been published in two installments in *Sail* magazine (May and June 1971), giving the information Ed would need to design the gear to fit our boat. It had been designed and built by James F. Ogg in California. Later we had read about a Cheoy Lee boat that had sailed from Massachusetts to England with a self-steering gear built from the same plans with some modifications. Ed suspected that "modification" meant "strengthening." That was what he wanted to do anyway, using stronger materials than those specified in the original plans. That, plus inflation, would make ours more expensive than Ogg's, but we thought we would still get a sturdier gear for less money than the currently available store-bought variety.

It was around this time that Jake Mottayaw began to think he had made a big mistake. He had agreed to make fiddles for our dinette table and the wooden rudder for the self-steering gear.

Tall, gentle, and prematurely gray-haired, Jake was a forester who loved trees and wood almost as much as he loved sailing his *Anna Maru*. In addition to being mayor of Fernandina, Jake worked for Container Corporation, and he and Anne, his wife, were the parents of three school-age children with the concomitant involvements. In Jake's "spare" time he produced miracles in wood—everything from small carvings of whales to furniture. As evidence of his generosity, soon every sailboat in Fernandina would have teak fiddles around its dinette table—except the *Anna Maru*.

Now he could escape us only by going to work. We met him at his house at five o'clock on workday afternoons, greeted him early on Saturday mornings in his garage, and on our weekend trips called him late Friday nights to announce cheerfully that we were back in town. He was our resident wood expert.

During the first week of our Christmas vacation we also enlisted the aid of a metal expert. Jake directed us to Clifford Mattox at Fabralloy, Inc., a large establishment that handled metal fabricating work for the local Rayonier and Container Corporation mills.

With our copies of *Sail* containing the plans for the self-steering gear and with Ed's calculations and specifications adapting their plans to our boat, we went to see Henry Wilt, president of

Fabralloy. He gave his clearance to our trifling project and took us to Mr. Mattox. Mr. Mattox was not a boat person. Ed explained the gear and what it was supposed to do and the stresses in terms of wind and weight of water to which it might be subjected. Mr. Mattox looked interested. But did he understand?

"Then that piece," he said, pointing to the plan, "acts like a trim tab."

"That's exactly what it is," Ed sighed his relief.

Mr. Mattox was not a boat person and probably had never heard of a self-steering gear for a small sailboat, but he was an engineer and he knew metals and he understood the principle. He also understood Ed's insistence on strength.

So the self-steering gear would be built in thirds. Ed did the math and bought the marine hardware and miscellaneous nuts and bolts. Jake would find the mahogany for the rudder, cut, laminate, and shape it and drill the necessary holes. Ed and I would varnish it. Mr. Mattox and Fabralloy would fabricate the stainless steel gears and the large, heavy stainless steel bracket that would attach the gear to *Folly*'s reverse stern.

At this point we had done everything we could for the self-steering gear, including naming it "Jake," so we turned our attention to everything else.

We went to Jacksonville and bought two modest pieces of teak that we had no trouble fitting into Sam's back seat. They cost us $51.95. Two modest pieces.

One of them was earmarked for our fiddles. When we had bought *Folly*, my two first orders were to put real fiddles on our table, replacing the ridiculous little moldings the factory had provided, and to throw away the red shag carpet. The carpet was still with us, but I was getting the fiddles.

Back in the Mottayaw garage, Jake sawed the moldings from the formica, and we thrashed out the plan for the new fiddles—strong, two-inch fiddles that would give some hope of keeping most things on the table. Once again we left the teak and the plan in the hands of our overworked expert.

There was another job that, in the interest of economy, we wanted to do ourselves. We needed strong, reliable grab rails inside the cabin—something Yankee Yachts had overlooked. We had measured the length of the main cabin, and at Graham's we found a long teak grab rail and a short one that, together, would provide the necessary length. We bought stainless steel wood screws and finishing washers for through-bolting the rails.

There has been some dispute about whether our beautiful, sturdy grab rails inside *Folly*'s cabin are the result of luck or skill. But on a cool December day I stood inside the cabin sweating, my eyes shut tight, as I held the rails in place while Ed drilled from the deck above me with an electric drill. Not once did he drill in the wrong place. Not once did the drill break through the side of the teak. The results were perfect. We congratulated ourselves, cleaned up the fiberglass drillings, and collapsed.

Now it was time to close up shop temporarily, pick up my mother in Waycross, and travel to Louisiana for Christmas with Ed's family. Mama Lormand still didn't know about our plans, and it was increasingly difficult for me to write chatty letters about our daily activities when most of our daily activities were related to Ed's voyage.

On the Saturday night after our arrival, Ed caught his father in a weak moment and Papa Lormand said, "Sure, go ahead and tell her."

"OK, I'll tell her tomorrow morning so you'll be here, too," Ed said.

"No, I won't be here," Papa Lormand said piously, "I have to go to church."

For what may have been the first time in all our years of marriage, Ed was up before I was the next morning. He told his mother about his plans while my mother was there to provide moral support. Papa Lormand returned from church after the deed was done.

Mama Lormand had been done an injustice. She took the news calmly—outwardly anyway. She had been listening to Ed's dreams for a long time, but of course, having a date set did cast things in a different light.

From then on we wrote Mama Lormand about our preparations, but it wasn't until the morning of June 9, when Ed had a chance to take her to the boat and show her *Folly*'s equipment and supplies, that she could say, "Now I feel better."

In some ways the anticipation was more difficult for Papa

Lormand. As Ed pointed out, he probably understood more about the real hazards involved. But both he and Mama Lormand supported us with their interest and hard work, and I was proud of them on June 10.

And Christmas brought Ed a Panasonic tape recorder and thirty hours of blank tapes and a Timex Quartz watch.

After our Louisiana holiday Ed and I returned to Fernandina for the remaining week of our vacation. When we got there, we ran errands before we went to the house to unpack.

We stopped by Fabralloy to give Mr. Mattox our home address and to tell him that Jake could show him the boat if he needed more information or measurements.

Then we went to Standard Hardware, one of my favorite places. It is a large marine hardware store that backs up to the Amelia River and that fits out and supplies Fernandina's fleet of shrimp boats. Most of the hardware was somewhat oversized for our purposes, but for some of our needs this was our best source, and we had been buying—as well as sightseeing—there since *Tippecanoe*. We had more than once found ourselves shopping just ahead of the owner of a fleet of shrimp boats, and we were pleased and amused when our order of $5 always received the same patient attention as the next man's order amounting to $500. At the same time Standard Hardware's no-frills, no-nonsense approach to a boat's needs was often a refreshing change from the usual yachtsman's store.

This time we bought oakum, cotton, and epoxy putty to go into Ed's hull-repair kit. We also priced bottom paint. We had learned of Britain's value-added tax that added 20 percent (then) to yacht supplies, and Ed intended to take with him enough paint for a bottom job.

As we were leaving, Ed pointed out that we would have to relay the final order for the bottom paint through Jake and that he could pick it up for us when it arrived. Between January and June we would be in Fernandina only on weekends, and Standard Hardware was closed on Saturdays. That thought was astonishing. Only five more months of weekends only.

Our salesman gave us his home telephone number. "If you need anything just before you leave, and we're closed, call me at home. I'll be glad to open the store for you," he offered.

This was typical Standard Hardware service in our experience. It was also another addition to our growing collection of friends, relatives, and tradespersons who seemed to take a special pleasure in helping us prepare for a real adventure.

We tackled one more holiday project before we returned to Atlanta and work (school work, that is). We went to Jacksonville to the Nautical Supply Company and bought Ed's charts. After about an hour and a half of poring over chart catalogs, we bought charts, light lists, tide tables, sight reduction tables, and the Nautical Almanacs for the United States East Coast and for the British Isles, including charts of Bermuda and the Azores, just in case.

We then went to see the local sailmaker, who sold us a piece of blue acrylic so that we could make a cover for the self-steering gear's wind vane.

Our sail inventory still was slim. We had the Johnson main and working jib that had come with *Folly* and the 150 percent Hood genoa that we had bought. A storm jib and trysail were necessities, and we would order them. We might not be able to afford more sails than that.

Between batches of cookies I was making for a reception for one of Ed's students, I delivered our sails to Vic Lipscomb, who would send them to Willie Poulsen of Eastern Shore Sails in Fairhope, Alabama. We wanted the stitching checked on the ones we had. We wanted another set of reefing points on the mainsail (to make two sets), and we wanted about eighteen inches of slave material stitched along both sides of the foot of the genoa for chafe protection. We also ordered the storm sails and asked (begged) that Poulsen send some spare material for possible patching and mending at sea.

At Nautical Supply in Jacksonville we had priced a set of International Signal Code flags. About $100. We went back to Atlanta, borrowed our friend Harriet Mitchum's sewing machine, found the flag dimensions in a supply catalog (I shouldn't have said that—they'll stop printing the dimensions) and bought the material. I measured and cut while Ed sewed. With Harriet's machine on a card table in our living room and scraps of red, white, blue, green, yellow, and black, we looked like Betsy Ross gone amok. Back in Fernandina Ed took a bunch of dowel pins to Jake's and cut toggles for raising the flags. Our flags cost between $20 and $25 and some time.

And we went out on the beach before breakfast on cold winter weekend mornings to take sextant shots with our plastic sextant. Plotted ourselves within a mile and a half of Sea Sand. Not bad.

Folly had to have a home when Ed arrived in England. Since Ed had to be back in Atlanta to teach in the fall term in September, *Folly* had to have a long-term berth. We planned then to sail her back to Fernandina the following summer. In the meantime we wanted to find a marina in Plymouth that would allow us to live aboard while we were there and that would agree to keep *Folly* with some sort of reasonable security until we could return.

It was a happy set of circumstances that led us to the Mayflower Marina. At the suggestion of the British Consulate in Atlanta, we wrote to the Plymouth Chamber of Commerce in November 1975, almost seven months before Ed's projected departure date, asking for names, addresses, and any other information that they could supply concerning yacht clubs, municipal docking facilities, and boatyards in the area. Dock space in our own home sailing area near Fernandina Beach ranged from scarce to nonexistent, so a seven-month head start did not seem excessive.

The Chamber of Commerce replied with a booklet containing information about clubs, marinas, boatyards, and Plymouth Harbor, and we wrote first to the Royal Western Yacht Club. The RWYC was not prepared to take long-term reservations, but the Sailing Secretary's helpful letter suggested that the Mayflower Marina could probably fill our needs. He also gave us an indication of the going rates, gave us the name of Blagdon's Boatyard in case we decided to lay *Folly* up ashore, and offered the facilities of the club and any other help that he could give us while we were in Plymouth. This generous attitude was the typical British response to all our questions and requests for help.

Our letter to the Mayflower Marina brought a prompt reply from the harbourmaster, who described the marina and its facilities, the fees, their insurance requirements, and their security arrangements. He also indicated that he had made a provisional booking for us beginning in late July. Now we had a home in England. In April we sent a draft for £25 as a deposit for our reservation.

I wrote Malvina Finlayson in Deal, Kent, giving her the name and description of *Folly* along with Ed's proposed route. She, in turn, would give the information to her brother in the Royal Navy and to Lloyd's. If any Royal Navy airplanes on routine maneuvers sighted Ed, we would get word from them, and Lloyd's had agreed to telephone Malvina if anyone reported Ed's position to them.

On a weekend in Atlanta we finished the flags, and I gave myself a crash course in celestial navigation. I was pretty good at the math but felt I could use a little more experience with the sextant. It was frivolous, perhaps, for me to spend time on that project, but after the apparently endless day-to-day plodding of our preparations, it gave me a great sense of specific accomplishment. Besides, I did not intend for Ed to singlehand forever.

Meanwhile, Jake was working hard in his garage. The teak fiddles were finished and the table was back aboard. But *Folly*'s companionway opened far too low in the cockpit. Any extended offshore cruising would require a bridge deck. Ed and Jake came up with a masterful bit of design and engineering, giving us a bridge deck, a compass box to house our Ritchie compass so that it would be visible from the tiller and also from the cabin, and a step down (far down) into the cabin. That step seemed like a real obstacle at first—another trade-off—but we soon got used to it and thought of it as Lormand's instant physical fitness program. The bridge deck and hatch board went home with us for painting.

During winter and spring quarters Ed's work at school was murderous. Besides teaching a full load in the Music Department (freshman and sophomore music theory plus the woodwind students), he was teaching college-level theory to a ten-year-old prodigy two nights a week, counterpoint classes at home twice a week to several of his college students who wanted them in preparation for transferring to other colleges, and his own private woodwind students at home. He was also teaching a theory class in the night division at the college two nights a week (for extra money) and practicing clarinet himself to stay in shape for a concert. There were times when mere survival until June 10 seemed in doubt.

We waited not so patiently as February wore on toward March and we still had no sails. But on an extra weekend at home Ed converted our small Ritchie compass (from the *1st Folly*) into a hand-bearing compass. And we went to Sears and bought two sleeping bags.

In the first week in March the spare parts for the Optimus stove arrived and our old sails returned—but no spare material for repairs. Sailmakers do not like to sell sailcloth. That would encourage sailors—already notoriously penurious, not to say cheap—to do their own sail work. We sent a message back to the sailmaker that unless he could make house calls in mid-Atlantic, we would need spare material.

The work he had done on the old sails was excellent. The new reefing points on the main and the slave material on the genny looked good, as did the Yankee 28 emblem and our identifying number 15 now on the mainsail. On Saturday, March 6, we went sailing to "try them out." The next day, Sunday, we had excellent intentions of spending a couple of hours cleaning *Folly* before starting home to Atlanta at a reasonable hour. Then we got to Dell's and saw that two of our sailboat neighbors were out sailing. We took a look at the blue sky and fresh northeast breeze, and our resolve crumbled. Thirty minutes later we were on our way out. *Folly* was dirty, but the breeze was cool and strong, and the genny pulled like a racehorse. The sun sparkled on the water. The whole day sparkled. And some days the soul just needs to go sailing.

The question of firearms aboard had been studied pro and con by early spring. Ed was not planning an armed attack anywhere, and he felt confident that our 37-mm flare gun (a gift from his father that we had carried aboard the *1st Folly*) would be sufficient to repel boarders, but he wanted something for discouraging sharks. Papa Lormand sent us his shotgun. That would save buying one and would serve the purpose. Ed prepared some of the shells to use simply for percussive effect. He could also use these shells to fire directly at the bridge of a ship to call its attention to imminent collision.

Jake kept building. Adding the bridge deck meant that our teak cockpit grate would have to go and a new one be built to fit the reduced cockpit. By the first week in April the new grate (made of marine plywood) was ready to be taken to Atlanta for painting. And Ed was beginning to make a wooden bracket that would hold our Panasonic radio with a slot behind it for the International Signal Code Book. The signal flags were in order in their custom-made (by Ed) case, tied to the mast in the cabin. Instead of creating another problem, we had solved two at once. We had a place to keep the flags, and we had transformed the mast into something interesting to look at in the cabin. Ed also built a cabinet at the foot of the quarter berth to hold books. The cabinet door was made of peg board to allow some air inside.

We shopped for quite a while before deciding on material for dodgers to fit along each side of the cockpit from upper lifeline to rail. We wanted them to provide easy identification with "Lormand's 2nd Folly" in big letters legible from some distance. Ed would need them for protection from the weather, and they must be substantial enough to survive the voyage. The material in fabric shops was not strong enough. An upholsterer showed us some plastic material that was supposed to last forever. We weren't convinced. We went back to Standard Hardware and bought heavy treated canvas. We measured and drew off two pieces and took the material to a shoe store to be cut and sewed. Ed did the lettering and painted on the name. The upholstery shop put in the grommets.

During the first weekend in April, Jake and Anne Mottayaw invited us to have dinner at their house two weeks later. I wrote to my mother, "I'm fascinated by people who can plan something two weeks in advance." It was very nearly our only social outing during the spring.

Ed conveniently had a birthday on April 20, giving everybody an excuse to make a donation to the cause. Mother gave him a pair of Topsider moccasins. Alec Jones gave him a pair of sea boots. I gave him six pairs of socks—three cotton and three wool—very glamorous. At least his feet might stay warm and dry.

Our instinct for parsimony was thriving. We brazenly accepted all gifts, loans of equipment and tools, and the free labor of friends. And we kept finding new ways to conserve our slim cash supply without compromising on the quality of any item that one's life or health might depend on.

We needed a harness to keep the cook from falling into the stove in a pitching galley. Ed had designed a good harness in one of his 325-mile sessions of meditation. In a chilly, misty rain in Fernandina we drove out to a junkyard on the edge of the marshes on the west side of the island. Ed explained our needs to the two men who guarded the derelict cars and household appliances. He told them about his sailboat over at Dell's Marina. He was going to sail her to England. Alone. Needed something to keep him off the stove. When he finished, the look in their eyes said quite clearly, "Let's do whatever he says and get him out of here before he gets violent."

They sold us two sets of seat belts for a dollar each if we would detach them from a car ourselves. The shoe store stitched each set together, making two belts with an "O" ring on each side. To the "O" rings Ed attached a length of nylon line with a hook on the end to fasten into the brass bails he had installed on either side of the galley. The cook could be held in place securely, and in case of a flareup on the stove, he could simply punch the button (behind his back) to open the belt and step away from the stove.

But in some places even we couldn't cut corners. Insurance was a necessity. We knew that many yachtsmen sailed without it because of its astonishing cost, taking the financial risk upon themselves. We didn't have that option even if we had been inclined to take it. At that time a bank in Jacksonville owned more of *Folly* than we did, and we doubted whether they would look favorably on Ed's setting out for England singlehanded and uninsured. To be honest, we were not absolutely sure that they wouldn't try to stop us even if we were fully covered. I had visions of arriving at our marina to find *Folly* surrounded by armed bank guards.

There was no way to carry on with adequate preparations in secret, and anyway, provisioning and setting sail under cover of darkness just wasn't our style. We had to be insured and we had to conduct our operations openly and take our chances. We made no announcement to our Florida banker of our intentions, but we asked Mac and Eileen Macauley, our U.S. insurance agents, if they could help us find an insurance company that would insure a singlehanded transatlantic crossing. We knew that the premium would be one of our major expenses, but we would protect our investment and the bank's investment and at least give that much evidence of responsibility in what the bank's board of directors would undoubtedly consider a patently irresponsible venture.

In June 1975 we talked to Mac and Eileen about our plans for the first time. By a stroke of pure luck we had stumbled on insurance agents who were infected immediately by an enthusiasm for our adventure that matched our own. They began scouting for an insurance company susceptible to the same disease. That was more difficult.

To help them in their task, they sent us a questionnaire to fill out with a sketchy resume of Ed's plans for preparing for the voyage. We submitted the answers on two single-spaced, typewritten pages. Mac and Eileen began their inquiries, and a lively correspondence began between us.

July 8, 1975
HI:
   What they are trying to do is discourage me; my progress report is no progress as yet. Most of the companies throw up their hands at the mere thought of a 28′ boat traveling that distance. I have submitted it to two new companies this date and will keep you posted.
Eileen.

July 17, 1975
HI:
   No success as yet. We are still working with our domestic companies; however, this week I ventured into the foreign market. Will keep you posted.
Eileen.

August 1, 1975
HI:
   ENCOURAGEMENT. We are corresponding with a company in

London, England, that specializes in yacht insurance. Will keep
you posted.
Eileen.

August 15, 1975
HI:
   Lloyd's has given us a quotation of $504, which is good for
thirty days, but no matter. All we are really looking for now is
market and this is the first positive response received to date.
   What's so ironic is the London Agency Office in Atlanta re-
fused even to quote on it.
Eileen.

Then in September Mac and Eileen got a reply from Edward
Lumley (Yacht Insurance) Limited in London. It was an iffy
thing. What any insurance company agreed to, provisionally, in
1975, could be denied in 1976. But if we could give them more
information, Lumley, as our agents, would be willing to try.
They asked five questions—or rather groups of questions—about
Ed's plans and preparations of himself, the boat, and equipment
for the voyage.
   One night we sat up in bed with our preliminary lists, specifications on the boat, and stacks of equipment brochures spread
around us, and Ed began dictating his answers. I typed them up
the next day and sent the report to the Macauleys. It ran to nine
single-spaced pages. At the time it was a tedious chore. It was
not until much later that we learned the full significance of our
detailed responses to those questions.
   Our final step in getting an insurance quote was to have *Folly*
surveyed. Mac and Eileen gave us the names of two surveyors in
Jacksonville whose surveys would be acceptable to insurance
companies. We wrote.
   In the meantime the press had discovered us. In March Joe
Caldwell, a reporter for the *Jacksonville Journal,* came to see us.
Joe's first article appeared on March 27. Another came out on
April 24. It soon became evident that there was considerable
general interest in a music teacher who wanted to sail the Atlantic alone on a twenty-eight-foot sailboat. The wire services
picked up the story, and sightseers began appearing on the dock
at Dell's. This was a mixed blessing. Ed was happy to talk to

everyone, but he was beginning to feel pushed to finish everything by his deadline.

There was no longer anything *sub rosa* about our activities if
there ever had been. When Eileen talked to the surveyor, Carl
Strocchi, to set up the appointment for us, he told her he had
read one of Joe's articles. Our Jacksonville banker had read it,
too. He pulled our file, found the name of our local insurance
agent, and called Eileen to express his understandable concern.
Eileen gave him every piece of positive information she could
think of and sent us a memo describing the exchange just to
keep us informed.

We met Mr. Strocchi aboard *Folly* on a Saturday early in
April. Afterward I wrote Eileen: "He inspected *Folly,* and Ed
bent the poor man's ear for about four hours. At the end of that
time, he seemed to think we are doing all the right things. He
said he would send you his report."

He did, and it was favorable. And Mac and Eileen prepared a
copy of the survey for the bank as further reassurance, along
with a copy of our correspondence with the Mayflower Marina
in Plymouth. The Mayflower Marina had its own requirements
for insurance, and we were being careful to arrange for coverage
that would satisfy their needs. We felt that all our efforts in this
direction gave clear indication that we were making firm plans
for *Folly*'s future and had no intention of abandoning her on
foreign shores. Eileen also wrote to assure our banker that the
bank would be shown as loss payee on the policy.

Before this packet of information could get into the mail, our
banker called Eileen. She described to him the information that
was on the way. He said that answered his questions.

We heard nothing from the bank until the first week in May.
Our banker telephoned Ed in Atlanta and asked that I sign a
standard bank guaranty form. I signed willingly. The bank now
had a warm body to deal with in the event that Ed vanished
forever over the horizon, and their officer wrote a nice note
thanking Ed for his cooperation and extending "best wishes for
a successful and happy voyage." The bank had never taken the
role of villain in our minds. Their uneasiness was certainly justified and understandable.

The final insurance quotes, when they came, were good and

bad. Lloyd's original quote of $504 had been based on a misun-
derstanding, and their new quote was $1,750 for fourteen
months. Whew!

Edward Lumley, however, had reduced their quote, after re-
viewing our survey, from $1,115.40 to $810.60, for $20,000 on
the hull and $100,000 third-party liability, with $500 deductible.
The decision was simple enough. We bit the bullet and mailed
the check. And to our surprise, when the policy arrived, we
discovered that we were now insured by Lloyd's with Edward
Lumley as agents. Does anyone understand the insurance business?

3

The "What-If's" and the Radio

Our day-to-day efforts continued. While Ed taught and practiced, I telephoned and wrote to equipment dealers and made innumerable trips to Lipscomb Sailboat Company and miscellaneous hardware stores.

Everything we could possibly get locally we bought from Vic Lipscomb who, realizing quite early the magnitude of our needs, had made a helpful financial arrangement with Ed. If Vic didn't have it or couldn't get it, we scoured the boat catalogs and advertisements in magazines and wrote for specifications and price quotes. We tried to arm our decision-making with as much information as possible and then we bought. And Ed's continuous teaching brought in enough cash to keep pace with the orders.

Boat gear filled our guest room and overflowed under the piano in the living room every two weeks, and then it was loaded into Sam for the trip south.

By far the greatest portion of the gear was made up of spares. Ed was teased about taking along enough spares to build a whole new boat at sea, but the captain was not perturbed. He spent every possible moment thinking of all the disasters that could possibly befall *Folly* at sea and then thinking of a solution. He visualized total loss of electrical power from the engine. In fact he considered this a probability, not just a possibility. Therefore he thought of *Folly*'s electrical system as a backup for the kerosene lights rather than vice versa. The galvanized kerosene running lights that we ordered were big-boat size, and the two kerosene lamps inside the cabin would provide enough light below for getting about and finding things as well as giving added light aboard at night to make *Folly* slightly more visible to other ships.

Ed also imagined *Folly* upside down and remembered reading that Sir Francis Chichester had narrowly escaped being knifed in a knockdown. He fitted *Folly*'s under-seat lockers with positive latches made with lengths of wooden dowels. Smaller dowels were used to make tiny cleats (another job for Jake's woodworking equipment). These were installed next to every drawer and sliding cabinet door with bits of nylon cord on the drawers and doors as tie-downs. The kind folk at Standard Hardware turned us loose in their scrap net bin and sold us pieces of shrimp net at a pittance per pound. We laced the net with shock cord and hooked it around every open shelf. By the time we finished this project, Ed felt that he was unlikely to be hit by anything harder than a bunk cushion.

What if Ed, connected by his safety harness, were washed overboard, then washed back to the boat, but because of the speed of the boat through the water could not get back to the point at which his harness was connected? He would carry his boat knife on a lanyard at all times.

What if a wave or gust of wind hit the boat just as Ed unhooked his harness—before he could hook on somewhere else? He put two lines on his harness. The second would be attached before the first was released.

What if a giant squid reached up from the deep, laying an inquisitive and monstrous tentacle over *Folly?* A machete was installed aboard to take care of the amputation.

What if, in mid-Atlantic, a beautiful young French girl in a bikini were put into a dinghy over the side of another sailboat carrying a man and another woman. One can imagine the circumstances. And what if the beautiful young French girl in the bikini rowed bravely over to *Folly* and begged Ed to rescue her? Could he, as a responsible seaman, leave the sweet young thing adrift and helpless? Could he, notwithstanding his persuasive powers, expect to convince me that the remainder of his voyage was chaste if not singlehanded? To the best of my knowledge he has never arrived at a wholly satisfactory solution to this one, but I helpfully pointed out that the young lady was very likely a co-conspirator in an imaginative hijacking plot.

While we were in the midst of all these "what-if's," we read somewhere that "lucky" people, as a group, characteristically were those who approached new ventures pessimistically, anticipating problems, examining consequences, and planning options and solutions. If so, we were manufacturing a lot of luck for ourselves.

In the same vein Ed began collecting supplies for our medical kit by going to his dentist, Dr. Charles McCrory, for his regular six-month checkup and by seeing his internist, Dr. Wai Yun Syn, for a routine physical.

"If I find something wrong," Dr. Syn asked, "will you change your plans?"

"Nope," Ed said.

Ed was healthy, and those two doctors along with Dr. Thomas W. Huff, Ed's periodontist and a close personal friend, agreed to help him compile a list of medical supplies similar to those carried by other long-distance sailors.

"If you were going to be two or three weeks away from medical help, what would *you* want aboard?" he asked them.

"Another dentist," Dr. McCrory replied quickly.

Dr. Syn answered, "Another doctor and a drugstore."

Our resulting medical kit was about three hundred dollars' worth of pessimism. Actually, it was worth more than that because our three friendly doctors contributed innumerable samples and several medical implements—grips for pulling teeth, syringes for giving injections, hemostats, bandages, plastic gloves, and on and on. They also generously donated their time in giving lessons on how to use the equipment, in the process helping Ed learn to suture and tie using one hand and his teeth. (What if he had a compound fracture of one arm and could use only one hand?) They went through the list of drugs, from vitamin pills to morphine, describing the circumstances that would warrant their use. They wrote prescriptions for drugs that could not be bought over the counter. I wrote everything down, putting the list of drugs and their uses in the red loose-leaf binder that Ed would take with him. When we tried to pay for the medicine, the instruments, and the extra time, our doctors refused, pointing out that they would make a fortune repairing the damage Ed would do to himself at sea with all that exotic equipment.

Their parting advice was to stay away from The Merck *Manual of Diagnosis and Therapy* (which Ed would also have aboard) unless he was actually sick or hurt because if he read it while he was well, he would soon imagine that he wasn't.

Our last health-related project was to go to the health department for shots. Ed asked the nurse what shots he would need for England.

"None," she answered.

"I might end up in Spain. Hurricane. Wrong turn. What if my navigation isn't as good as I think it is?" Ed said.

The nurse looked puzzled.

"Northern Africa," I suggested. "What shots would he need if he went to Africa?"

The nurse looked irritated. Hands on her hips, she gave Ed her best head-nurse stare. "You've *got* to know where you're going," she snapped.

Ed took pity and explained. She relented and gave him a smallpox vaccination and the tetanus shot Dr. Syn had recommended.

The food list was my job. In making decisions about food, I consulted the only experts I knew—other singlehanders. I gathered all their books and studied their lists. They were helpful and gave me some ideas, but most of them were British and had different sorts of food available to them and different tastes. In the end I was on my own.

I sat down at our dining table one day with my yellow legal pad and started estimating a reasonable quantity of food for a 138-pound male for 120 days.

"It does not take 120 days to sail from Florida to England," you may be saying. Our answer? But what if *Folly* were dismasted—rudderless? Then how long would it take?

So I was thinking in terms of 120 days—90, anyway. I began

by jotting down menus. Breakfast. Lunch. Dinner. Teatime. Happy hour. Day #1: Sandwiches—beef stew. Then I began to laugh. What if day #10 directed Ed to produce all sorts of culinary gems when he was standing on his ear in a gale? I threw out the first yellow page and started over.

In the end I counted meat dishes, vegetables, fruits, juices, breakfast foods, and snacks. I took a wild guess at amounts of rice, biscuit mix, sugar, coffee, and other staples, erring on the side of oversupply.

With the exception of things like powdered milk, instant soup mix, and a few packages of powdered eggs, most of the food was canned. Water had to come from somewhere for reconstituting, and with a limited fresh-water supply, it seemed sensible to carry as many foods as possible that did not make demands on it. Fresh fruit and vegetables would be put aboard in quantities that could be expected to last until eaten. Some thought was also given to providing a variety of flavors and textures. Jars of nuts and corn to pop would be a relief from soft canned food. Ed likes corn chips and pig skins, too, but in the end few were put aboard because they took up too much space in relation to their food value.

Unfortunately, the most economical way to buy canned food was in large cans—inconvenient for a singlehander. To help solve this problem, Fred Steedley, who had bought my father's drugstore, offered to order single-serving cans of soups, stews, and fruit juices. He also ordered individually packaged mayonnaise and crackers. By buying through Fred, we could save a few cents per can on small sizes. We ordered a case of each flavor we wanted.

Gertrude ("Gert") Adams, a good friend and frequent crew, offered to get the eggs—six dozen freshly laid, never refrigerated eggs. The eggs had to be treated to encourage their survival in edible state for several weeks without refrigeration. The cans had to be treated to protect them from salt water and salt air. We had read about several methods of accomplishing this. We picked the anhydrous lanolin method for the cans. Each can was marked with waterproof markers to identify the contents, all paper labels were removed, and the cans were thoroughly coated with the stiff, gummy lanolin. A fringe benefit was the

marvelously softening effect this work had on the hands, and Ed
reported later that his morning fruit juice, drunk straight from
the can, gave his lips a protective coating.

For the eggs, we had read about two methods that we thought
were reasonable. Some people dunked the eggs one at a time
into rapidly boiling water for about five to ten seconds. Some
people gave each egg a thin coating of vaseline. Both methods
presumably provided the eggs with an airtight seal. In our usual
attitude of supercaution, we decided it wouldn't hurt if we used
both methods. One dozen eggs would be put aboard already
hard-boiled. We gave them a vaseline treatment, too.

Unfortunately, the captain was no cook. In our sixteen years
of marriage, he had thought of the kitchen as an area one passed
through quickly on the way to the back door. But cooking on the
boat was different. It was one of the intriguing challenges of
singlehanding. He was interested in my research into the subject,
and he joined me in examining the possibilities. When we were
aboard *Folly,* he occasionally practiced, though bedeviled by my
unwelcome advice.

I put a Bisquick Cookbook aboard and also Janet Groene's
Cooking on the Go because of its wealth of suggestions for cooks
who work in small-boat galleys with a two-burner stove, limited
space, and no refrigeration. In addition, I wrote directions for
basic cooking in the loose-leaf notebook that contained the list
of food and medical supplies and their locations. I gave detailed
instructions for making coffee, rice, pancakes, and biscuits, and
for baking cornbread in the skillet. Ed, a Louisianan, loved
rice—the regular, long-cooking kind. Over the years I had de-
vised a method for cooking it that worked as easily on *Folly*'s
alcohol stove as it did at home. The different flavors of canned
food that could be poured over rice should provide variety as
well as vitamins.

Cigars ranked in importance just below food and water on
Ed's list of supplies. He smoked Swisher Sweets, the cheapest
(sorry, I mean least expensive, of course) cigar he could find,
and he smoked about ten of them a day. Swisher Sweets were
made at the King Edward Cigar Factory in Waycross, my home-
town. Peggy Wilson, who lived there and who had been my
friend since the beginning of time, agreed to pick up the cigars—

good fresh ones—and deliver them to Fernandina. Ed had decided that six hundred was a nice round number. If it looked as though the voyage would take longer than sixty days, he would just have to ration them. Peggy's son Mike drove twelve boxes of cigars to Fernandina the weekend before Ed's departure, and Mama Lormand, Gert, and whoever else had a free moment sealed each box in a plastic bag.

A perennial question, from both boating and nonboating people, was, "What kind of radio will you carry?"

Ed's answer—"A Zenith Transoceanic if I can afford one," before we bought our radio, and "A Panasonic Tech 1100," after we had bought it—was not satisfactory.

"No, I mean what kind of transmitter."

"An ELT. It sends out an SOS on a frequency that's monitored by commercial aircraft." He still was missing the point.

"But how will you talk to people? Contact Fran? Send for help?"

"I won't."

At that, Ed's questioner would look at me, obviously thinking, "If she's standing there quietly listening to this, she's as crazy as he is."

Ed would then try to explain his thoughts on the subject of radios on small boats at sea. He was not adamantly opposed to them. We had been aboard Tommy Hall's *Libtom III* once, anchored in a remote creek off the Intracoastal Waterway, and Tommy had called Elizabeth, his wife, on his radiotelephone. Telephoning someone from a small boat in the middle of nowhere was very entertaining. Certainly it would be at sea. The next night, even closer to home, Tommy tried to call Elizabeth again. Couldn't get through. The radio was dry and the weather was good.

A radio on a twenty-eight foot boat in the North Atlantic would very likely get wet. Even before it got wet, the sort of radio that we might be able to afford would have a range of something like forty miles. Ed and *Folly* would be farther away from land than that on the first night. He could, however, communicate with ships, possibly patch calls through, and at least have some assurance of having his position reported occasionally to the U.S. Coast Guard, Lloyd's, or me—as long as the radio stayed dry and/or worked. On the other hand, a primary and vital aim of a singlehander is to stay as far away from shipping lanes as possible.

To help ensure that the radio stayed operative, Ed would have to maintain an adequate power supply. That would mean carrying extra gasoline for running the engine to keep the battery equal to that kind of drain. It could mean finding a place for an additional or bigger battery. Without a radio or other excessive battery-draining device, our existing battery and twenty-gallon gasoline tank would be sufficient. Ed could use the engine to get in and out of port and run it for ten or fifteen minutes every three days in order to keep the battery charged enough to start the engine and supply the cabin lights, compass light, electric running lights, and even spreader lights as backups to the kerosene system. Considering all these aspects of the situation, the advantages of carrying a radio were whittled away somewhat by the disadvantages.

There were two other reasons for Ed's decision. One was psychological. If I—or Ed's mother—expected to hear from him regularly—or even irregularly—while he was at sea, or if I had some reasonable expectation of getting position reports from ships, then not hearing anything could be unnerving. I agreed with the assessment in theory, but I did not appreciate it fully until much later.

The other reason was based on Ed's profound conviction concerning the responsibility of a singlehander. Anyone who sailed away from a dock alone on a small boat to cross an ocean automatically raised the odds against arriving anywhere safely. If he fell overboard, Jake, the self-steerer, would sail *Folly* merrily away without a backward glance. If he were hurt or ill, there would be no one to take over. When he slept, there was no one to stand watch—Jake was notoriously shortsighted. And a certain amount of time, unavoidably, would be spent in shipping lanes in which a large ship could appear over the horizon and be upon a small sailboat in a matter of fifteen minutes, running her down without ever being aware of a collision.

The risks and responsibilities of a lone sailor were entirely different from those of a sailor with a crew aboard. A crew increased the safety factor for the captain, and a captain, in turn, had some responsibility for the safety of his crew. In case of trouble he had not only the right but an obligation to do everything possible to get help from the Coast Guard, from any other rescue service, or from another pleasure boat or commercial vessel within calling range.

But Ed believed devoutly that anyone who voluntarily took the extraordinary risk of sailing away from a dock singlehanded could risk his own life if he wanted to, but had absolutely no right to risk the life of someone else—or of someone else's son. He didn't relish living with the memory that he had called for help at sea and that someone else had died in the rescue effort. In fact he had decided that he would activate the ELT only if he were forced into his life raft and convinced that he faced certain death. A call for help would not be frivolous. He had occasion later to test his resolve.

All these considerations buried a radiotelephone so far down on our list of priorities that we thought of it only when someone else brought up the question, and we knew that our budget would never stretch to include one.

4

Departure

We postponed several major equipment purchases until the last possible moment for economic reasons. We had met our day-to-day expenditures—which were considerable—for equipment and building materials, but we still had to buy a life raft, a good sextant, and a good suit of foul weather gear, and pay Fabralloy for their work on the self-steering gear and Graham's for the last bottom painting. Our neighborhood banker in Atlanta, in spite of the fact that she was fully informed about Ed's plans, arranged for a loan that would cover these expenses. We had done the research. We knew what we wanted and where we were likely to get the best buy, so we rushed to order.

We had decided on an Avon four-man life raft with a Series E survival pack. After numerous letters to dealers and distributors, we had almost given up trying to get any discount. We did get one interesting quote, but I found that I had neglected to mention in my letter the fact that we wanted the raft in the fiberglass canister and not in a soft valise. The new quote was discouraging.

Then we talked to Herb Piker, the salesman through whom we had bought *Folly.* Herb now was running his own yacht brokerage firm, Ortega Yacht Sales, in Jacksonville. He said that he could get the life raft we wanted for whatever it cost him, saving us at least a couple of hundred dollars. We said, "Super. Get it."

After years of researching sextants, Ed had decided that a small sextant with only a three-power scope would best suit his needs. On a small sailboat a four-power scope would make the horizon excessively jumpy. It would not make an accurate shot impossible, but it would make it more difficult. Besides, a small, three-power sextant would almost fit our budget. We ordered the O.S.K. 81B (small type) micrometer sextant from Goldberg's Marine, a discount marine supply company.

The sextant arrived about a month before departure time, and its quality was a pleasant surprise. Our plastic Davis sextant would be a good backup. The life raft arrived and was installed on *Folly*'s deck between the mast and the companionway hatch the Saturday before Ed was to leave.

The Atlantis foul weather gear, when it came, lived up to our high expectations. It actually felt comfortable to wear, and according to reports from users, it also kept sailors dry.

The suspense about the self-steering gear increased daily. Jake had finished the rudder and trim tab. Ed and I had varnished them. We had also finished the wind vane, complete with its three-pound counterweight, made of sheet lead melted on our kitchen stove and molded in a V-8 juice can. (I still find the distinctive ridges on that weight a pleasing aesthetic touch.) Harriet Mitchum had courageously cut and stitched the fitted acrylic cover for the vane.

Then time passed. Fabralloy, in whose hands rested the stainless steel gears and bracket, was a big concern. To do a job as small as ours, Mr. Mattox had to work on it after hours and on weekends. He didn't complain, but it took a while. June 10 was getting closer. Jake began getting nervous. After all, the gear was to be named for him—for all those hours of patient labor and moral support—and its success was crucial.

Four weekends before Ed was to leave, the stainless steel parts also were finished, but since we wouldn't have a chance to try the gear out until after our trip to Graham's for bottom painting, we decided to wait until our return to Fernandina to install the

Folly *at Graham Boat Yard, Jacksonville, Florida, for her last haul-out before "Jake," the self-steering gear, was installed in 1976.* (Jacksonville Journal, *Joe Caldwell photo)*

bracket and the gear on the boat. That way it could cause no problem during the haulout. Also, that way we would have a chance to try it—once—on the weekend before Ed was to set sail.

"What if it doesn't work?" Jake asked.

"It will work," Ed said.

The day they put the huge bracket on the stern, secured firmly with stainless steel backing plates inside the hull, I left town. I had to pick up some last-minute bits of equipment—really important things like self-destruct toilet paper and chemical for the head, which Ed would probably not use anyway as he favors a bucket at sea. At any rate, I effected my cowardly escape, and when I returned, the deed was done. Just aft of *Folly* I saw the blue acrylic wind vane, with "Jake" in white lettering, swinging in the breeze. Ed and both Jakes seemed to have survived.

The next day—Sunday, June 6—Ed, Jake, Little John May, and I took *Folly* out for the final sea trial. Little John was a college student with a summer job at Container Corporation. He had quickly endeared himself to Fernandina's sailing community by his willingness to be hoisted to the top of a mast to do lofty chores, by his trim physique (the better to hoist), and by his apparent eagerness to take his pay in invitations to go sailing. His cheerful and helpful presence had eased many of our more burdensome chores, and we were delighted to have an excuse to "pay" him now.

We motor-sailed out to the Sound, headed out to sea between the jetties, cut the engine, and set the gear. Hands off. All eyes on the compass. Steady as she goes. We began to feel the first faint ocean swells. There was a nice breeze. "Jake" was holding *Folly* on a reach straight out toward the sea buoy.

Jake took a deep breath—the Jake who does that—and went up to the bow. Ed followed him. Little John sat on deck next to the companionway hatch. I went below to get the camera to take a picture of our new helmsman and our lazy crew. "Jake" was holding a better compass course than any of us could have done. We tried several points of sailing with the same results.

"Had to work," Ed said. "My measurements were right, and Jake and Mr. Mattox did precisely what I asked. And besides that, we don't have time to do it all over again."

"It's probably the only thing ever made by a committee that worked," I commented.

Reluctantly we came about to sail home again. We had had a good excuse to go sailing, but there was more work to be done. Only four more days.

At this time I wrote in my log: "Have now given up setting and drying my hair. That saves me 50 or 55 minutes three times a week. First I gave up my morning exercise routine. That's 15 minutes a day. Then I gave up my walks. That's 40 minutes a day. I may be a slob, but I think we'll be ready by the 10th."

Ed's father had taken his vacation in order to be able to help during the last week, and Gert, a teacher, had gone to Fernandina as soon as her school year was over to help us, too. She brought the eggs. She and Ed's mother helped grease the last cans with lanolin. I treated the eggs. Papa Lormand built wooden brackets for the kerosene bow and stern lights. Whoever had a free hand at the proper time painted the brackets. My mother provided regular meals for which we appeared less and less regularly. Frantically we began stowing food and supplies aboard.

Ed and I had to return to Atlanta on Sunday night, June 6, so that Ed could give his exams and turn in grades. We wouldn't be back until Wednesday afternoon. Ed was setting sail at 10:00 A.M. Thursday. Everyone left at Fernandina had a list of things to do between Sunday night and Wednesday afternoon. For Ed and me the next five days were a blur of exhaustion.

We got home at three o'clock that Monday morning and slept three hours until school time. Then Ed got a call from radio station KIRO in Seattle, Washington. A report of his plans had gone out over the wire services. The radio station wanted to do a live interview by telephone that morning. Apparently they read the wire service news each morning and picked out the freak of the week to call for an interview. Ed readily agreed and enjoyed doing it even in his groggy state.

Then a local county newspaper editor called. Here we were, just around the corner. Why hadn't they heard something before? Could we come to his office for an interview? We went. The editor talked to us. He was interested, but slightly baffled.

"I don't even know what questions to ask," he said.

I have since thought that it was admirable of him to say that. In the following months Ed and I were often asked many questions by people who did not know what questions to ask.

The next two days passed somehow. We packed Sam to the eyebrows one last time and drove south.

The hours from 3:00 P.M. on Wednesday, June 9, when we arrived in Fernandina, until 10:00 A.M. on Thursday, June 10, were an unmitigated nightmare. Those we had left behind had done their best. But in the few remaining hours kerosene, water, and stove alcohol had to be put in their respective containers and lashed down. The cushions were propped back from the V-berths in the forward cabin and holes drilled in the fiberglass underneath to accommodate the 3/16-inch nylon line we used to lash the three-gallon plastic containers—cheap, three-gallon plastic containers. We had a lot of help, but Ed, who had spent years planning the details of this voyage, would often have to stop to explain why he wanted things done a certain way. There was no time for explanations. We needed simple obedience.

Clothes for warm weather and sun protection and clothes for cool weather had to be selected and packed. The medical supplies had to be packed in watertight (we hoped) plastic boxes, each labeled with a list of its contents. The last of the food had to be put aboard. And the combination list and diagram of all food, supplies, and clothing had to be finished so that Ed would be able to find what he needed. He was so busy drilling, filling, and lashing that he had no time to pay attention to what Gert and I were doing. I suggested that the red notebook containing all the lists should be first on his reading list.

As the sun set and darkness began complicating our work, *Folly*'s cabin looked more and more discouraging. Everything Ed would need seemed to be under something else. All our years of planning and organization were being canceled out by the press of getting these last supplies aboard. We were working so hurriedly that we were no longer packing efficiently. When the clothes went aboard, I told Ed that he would never wear everything I had packed, but I didn't have time to decide just what he would need.

More friends came down to the boat to help as they got off from work in the afternoon. And since we were now tied up at the city dock, many came simply to watch the frenzy.

A local newspaper man came for an interview. He sat in the companionway and asked his questions while Ed worked. Ed's mother came to the boat to watch. Ed showed her what he could of the many safety precautions *Folly* carried. The work could not slow down. More people came to watch and help. Our preparations were exciting, interesting, and amusing—to them. People cracked jokes. They were no longer funny. Nothing was funny any more. We just worked on. By midnight all of us were exhausted, and we couldn't stop.

At about 4:30 on Thursday morning Gert, Ed, Little John, and I were still working. We had almost reduced the chaos to proportions that we might be able to deal with between 7:00 and 10:00 A.M. Ed, Gert, and I went home. Little John miraculously found a space big enough to stretch out in. He would take a nap aboard, guarding *Folly*.

Ed and I crawled into bed and fell asleep as the sun was coming up. An hour and a half later the alarm went off. Up again and back to *Folly*. Ed went to the boat while I packed food that could go aboard already prepared. Ed would be busy for the first day or two, and he would have to watch for shipping. I made sandwiches and a thermos of coffee for the first day. Earlier in the week I had baked a batch of oatmeal cookies. My mother had made a bag full of biscuits. I cooked rice and put it in a plastic container. It would keep several days, and if Ed heated some stew, he could just throw in several spoonfuls of rice and have a meal of sorts.

When I arrived at the dock, a crowd had already gathered. It was a heartwarming crowd of friends and strangers come to wish Ed well and watch him set sail. Barbara Thornton, one of our dockmasters, helped him fill the gas tank. Father Brian came down and gave his blessing. Ed's parents, my mother, Ed, and I crowded into the dockmaster's house for a brief, private farewell. Then Ed was back aboard *Folly*. I cast off his dockline and ran to find the *Anna Maru*. Jake and Anne had offered to take Mother and me out to the sea buoy to see Ed off. My friend Peggy had come from Waycross for the occasion and would sail

Ed, Fran, and "Jake" shortly before Folly's *first voyage in 1976.*
(Jacksonville Journal, *Joe Caldwell, UPI photo*)

out with us. Ed's parents were going out on Tommy and Elizabeth's *Libtom III*.

There was a mild northeast breeze, and the day was slightly overcast. A breeze from any other direction at all would have been a lot better, but the weather wasn't violent so far. The northeast breeze would make the Gulf Stream very bumpy, and we could have hoped for a smoother beginning. A lot of things in the cabin were not yet stowed securely. We had just done the best we could with the time we had, and Ed was not inclined to postpone his departure.

Folly sailed out so beautifully that Ed had to wait for the rest of us in the Sound. The *Libtom III* and the *Anna Maru* sailed out with him to the sea buoy marking the St. Mary's Entrance. We took pictures, gave Ed a good-bye wave, and turned back toward Fernandina. Before we were halfway in, *Folly* had vanished over the horizon.

The breeze was cool and steady even though it was from the wrong direction. The sail back in was beautiful.

"How do you feel?" someone asked me.

"Relieved," I answered.

Ed had work to do in the cabin yet, and I knew that he was exhausted, but we had set a date and time and put the thing together. Ed had cast off the docklines at 9:58 A.M. on June 10, 1976, and in my own mind just getting *Folly* away from the dock was a major accomplishment.

"Aren't you worried?" someone else asked—and many would ask again.

"I can't. It wouldn't do any good." I was too tired to worry anyway.

PART 2

1976
Voyage

5

Logs, Tapes, and Recollections

DAY 1: *THURSDAY, JUNE 10*

Moments before leaving I ran up the jib and rolled and tied it to
the headstay with light string. The main was ready to hoist. I
started the engine to warm it up. I took the bow line back to the
cockpit, and Fran threw me the stern line. As soon as I had
cleared the dock, I pulled on the jib sheet, popping the jib open.
I set Jake and then went forward and hoisted the main. This
done, I looked back at the dock and saw people running for
Tommy's and Jake's boats. I took the engine out of gear and
sailed back and forth near the dock while my escorts came out
and joined me.

During these first few moments under sail, I realized that this
was the first time I had ever been alone sailing aboard *Folly*. All
my previous singlehanding experience had been with crew
aboard observing. This feeling of achievement, of having a boat
fully equipped for an ocean passage and being completely responsible and in command, was in itself worth all the pains of
months of preparations—this coupled with leaving two minutes
ahead of schedule.

Once Jake and Tommy joined me, I continued to motor until I was opposite Container Corporation, where I shut off the power. A group of Boy Scouts on the beach of Tiger Island dipped their ensign as I entered Cumberland Sound. Their salute was very moving.

My adrenalin was pumping as hard as it's ever pumped. I felt as though I had a great deal of physical strength. The only thing I worried about was the feeling of others around me. I was acutely aware that I had been a little short-tempered with a lady reporter before leaving, and I knew Fran was very tired.

I made two runs across Cumberland Sound waiting for the others to catch up. The sail out through the jetties was a pleasure as the swell of the ocean caught the boat. I set up a makeshift Bimini top and sat next to the mast organizing and securing all the halyards. Watching *Folly* perform without my help was my most exhilarating experience ever on the boat.

Log:

Noon position 30°40′N, 81°22′W, St. Mary's Buoy. Fuel 18 gallons. Water 60.

1600   Spotted first ship. Freighter going south.

Tape:

I set the taffrail log at the St. Mary's sea buoy. While uncoiling the seventy-five feet of line with the spinner attached for the log, I felt that win, lose, or draw, to have gotten to sea singlehanded, fully equipped, was in itself a large success and an accomplishment I would be proud of all my life. No matter what the results, the only people qualified to criticize my performance are those who have equipped a boat and traveled the same number of miles I have, and with each mile I put under the keel, the people who can do this become fewer and fewer.

My best heading is approximately 100 degrees. As soon as the other boats disappeared below the horizon, I sat down and ate a ham sandwich you sent out with me. As I watched land disappear, the fatigue of the past few days and the tension of the forthcoming unknown hit me. My arms felt like lead.

I napped sitting up in the cockpit for thirty minutes at a time,

Folly's *departure on the first voyage—June 10, 1976.* (Jacksonville
Journal, *Joe Caldwell, UPI photo)*

off and on, and hoped to see a fishing boat—someone I might know—returning to Fernandina, but none appeared.

Typical afternoon thundershowers passed but were quite moderate. About 1800 I began to cross the southbound shipping lane. Within an hour and a half I had crossed it. By 2200 I was entering the western edge of the Gulf Stream and could definitely feel an increase in the size of the wave action as we had wind against current. I also had to keep a very sharp lookout for northbound shipping traffic which, fortunately, I could spot in the distance, never on a collision course or approaching closer than two miles.

It is a dark night. I'm very tired but can't sleep for fear of being run down, and I'm constantly on guard for approaching squalls. We have had two during the night. Everything seems exaggerated, and the events of this night, my very first at sea singlehanding, have been an excellent initiation to Gulf Stream sailing. The ride is rough. Progress is rather slow but very exhilarating and at times bordering on the terrifying—the tension and anxiety are as great as I have ever felt in my life before. With every hour that passes my confidence grows in what *Folly* can bear. At dark I lit the kerosene bow light and stern light, and I've had nothing to do but stand watch while Jake sails *Folly* at her best.

Fran's Log:

You've been gone (from the sea buoy) almost twelve hours, and already there's so much I want to tell you I could write volumes. That might be the hardest part—not having you here to share everything with.

I thought the whole occasion this morning was just right. It was a warm gathering of friends, and everybody on the dock was enjoying it. Channel 4's news coverage of your departure was good. Their quotes from you were typical, and somehow they captured the flavor of the day.

After we got back home, Anne Mottayaw told me Barbara Thornton had called them to say you had forgotten to pay for the gasoline. She thought of it just as you were leaving and decided it would be indelicate to rush down to the boat waving the bill at you. I thought that was pretty funny. I'll settle up in the morning when I pay the dock fee.

My mind has been running on two cylinders all day, and now those have stopped. I hope you've been able to get a little sleep. I saw on the weather map on TV that you've sailed right into a low pressure area, but maybe it isn't too severe.

DAY 2: *FRIDAY, JUNE 11*

Log:

Noon position 30°55′N, 80°24′W. Day's run 65. Overcast. No sextant shots.

Tape:

1810. I've been busy since the last time I taped. As of noon today I was fifty-five miles offshore—pretty close to course. It's been hard to head too much north of 110° because of the northeaster. We were becalmed a couple of hours this morning, though, and we've had a variety of weather.

I haven't cooked. I've eaten bananas and some of your cookies, the two ham sandwiches you sent, a can of pudding, a few biscuits, and some powdered milk with Ovaltine. My water consumption is pretty good, I think. I'll be able to keep it right at a half gallon a day, and I have some extra water—plenty, if it will just stay fresh for me. I haven't missed ice at all. In fact everything tastes cool to me. The only liquor I've had so far is one beer last night, and I didn't drink it all.

The log seems to be working all right, and I'm really proud of that. And *Folly* handles herself well. If only the wind will veer, I can get out and head more toward the north. I'm afraid to head north now because of getting close to shore again. I'm just counting on the northerly drift of the current to help out. At the rate we're going, it could take me more than sixty days to make the trip. I tried steering myself, and I can't do any better than Jake can.

I know we're well away from Jacksonville now because I don't pick up the good radio station any more. I'm getting a Savannah station. When I left, I played the radio for about seven hours before I shut it down. I was in no mood to be really alone. My nerve ends tingled. Just tired. But I'm feeling much better today. I catnapped throughout the evening, and I've seen only two ships—the one yesterday and another just over the horizon today going north. I must be well out clear of the northbound traffic lane now.

The dodgers work well. They keep the wind off me. The running lights worked fine last night—burned all night. I refilled them this morning. I used just one cabin lamp. I'll use it tonight to see if it will work two nights in a row without refilling. I turned off the binnacle light when it occurred to me that Jake really didn't need it. I just used the penlight when I wanted to check the compass.

I keep the logbook on the hour, but I haven't kept it every hour because that gets to be a chore after a while. I should be in pretty good shape, though, running up and down the companionway. I came out of the cabin only once without hooking my harness on. When I noticed I hadn't hooked on, I quickly snapped it back, but I'll have to be very careful with that.

I thought everybody was really nice when I left, and I hope I didn't come off a fool with the reporters. I was trying to do the best I could, but I was tired. We had had a rough night. I was sorry to leave you that way, too. I had hoped we could get a good night's rest and everything, but it just couldn't be done. Dad had worked hard too. You don't know how much I appreciate it. Now if I can just do this well—just hold up and get there decently, then it won't be all for nothing.

It's funny how I go through different emotional stages. I have a few moments of despair when the boat won't go right, and I'm elated when it goes a little bit right. The weather gets gloomy, and I think about that a little, and all of a sudden I notice it's bright, and it's a beautiful day. I'm aware of the changes out here a lot more than on land, and I feel at peace with the sea. I'm more relaxed now than I was before I left because I felt a lot of tension wanting to get away, and I'm happy that I got away on time.

I miss you terribly. It's going to be that way, and I know that. I hope you get along just fine back home by yourself. It's a dirty trick with all the bills and everything coming, but I'm hoping you'll be able to manage. I've been running you silly all year. It's quite a project equipping a boat. I can't say it was more than I thought it would be, but it was as much as I thought. I wasn't disappointed in the number of things that had to get done. And just judging from everybody's questions, I think we actually thought of everything and got it done as it should have been. I was proud of the way we handled ourselves.

It's exciting doing this—exciting for me because I get to go out and do it. When we get to England, I'll make it up to you.

Somebody put a picture of you on the table. It was taken with a Polaroid just before I left, I think. It looks nice. I hope my being away so long won't make you think, "Oh my God, sixteen years of messing with that fool." But I know you'll be happy to see me and *Folly* again. I hope you aren't worrying.

Fran's Log:

I sent a message at eight o'clock—that I love you and I'm feeling fine. I sent it over and over again as I sat on the porch and looked over the ocean in your direction.

If these two days are any indication—and they may not be— I'm reacting the way I thought I would. My worry thoughts are because I don't know exactly where you are or what has been happening or—more important—how you feel about what's been happening. My mind refuses to accept thoughts of disasters— only happy thoughts of you out there trying things out.

I feel very proud of you for having the brains and the imagination and the strength of spirit to want to find your adventure. And right now I just hope you aren't too soaked and that *Folly's* cabin isn't a shambles. I keep reminding myself that the weatherman called it a *"weak* low pressure area," but I'll bet a weak one in the Gulf Stream can make it plenty bumpy.

DAY 3: *SATURDAY, JUNE 12*

Log:

    Noon position (1730) 31°55′N, 78°35′W. Day's run 74.

Tape:

    1958. I'm having my second beer of the voyage during this taping session. Today was the first totally clear day. The weather has been comfortable. I opened the forward hatch and discovered two stowaways—the most vicious houseflies I have ever encountered. The food must be well protected in baggies because the only place they can find a meal is on my hide. During combat in the past twenty-four hours I mortally wounded one in self-defense and am a bit hesitant about killing the second one because it may be my only companion for fifty days or more. I'm paying a greater price at sea for companionship than I ever paid with the closest of friends on land.

    I'm listening to Wilmington, North Carolina, on FM, verifying that I am in that area. I shifted over to a northerly track and traveled until I was east-northeast of Savannah, and then I headed east again, trying to stay in the Gulf Stream. My noon sight put me about 60 miles east of Savannah so I had to make more easting to get around Cape Hatteras. The wind has switched to the west, and Jake is doing fine. And now that the wind is more with the Stream, the ride is becoming very pleasant.

    I'm surprised at the variety of the weather. Becalmed is the worst, with the banging of gear and the heat during the day. I'm down to shorts only. Broke out the suntan lotion and sunglasses—I feel like a tourist.

    I am feeling much more rested, and my spirits are much higher. During the night I slept one-hour intervals—five or six hours all told. This routine isn't so bad as I expected, and I can be wide awake after one hour's sleep very quickly. I've forgotten about life on land except that I now realize that I don't have to go to work in the morning. That's a very good feeling.

    I've reached the conclusion that it takes a lot more energy to complete a given task at sea than it does on land. In a way this is good because small tasks use enough of my energy so that I don't suffer withdrawal pains from the fast pace we kept ashore. I've learned to do things slower. Today I have washed dishes and filled the running lights and cabin lights with real kerosene. The scented lamp oil supply is exhausted, but I don't find the kerosene smell offensive. I had to clean soot from the running lights because the flame had been a little too high.

I also went forward and sorted out fruit. The bananas are now hanging in a net slung from the port grab rail. I've eaten half a dozen, but today I noticed the ripening process is accelerating. There are about half a dozen left, and until I finish them, it will be a race between belly and time. Belly will win in the end. All the bananas will be saved. I've taken the carrots out of a plastic bag and put them in a net to air. I made an egg salad sandwich and milk for lunch and then ate another boiled egg.

I'm feeling more confident with the sextant, but shooting a sextant from a small boat is a real challenge—especially in the Gulf Stream where, even when becalmed, the wave action is severe.

Today I spotted a series of unbroken waves covering the horizon. They were two or three feet higher than the normal waves, and there were four or five of them approximately a minute and a half apart. When the waves passed under the boat, I could look down them, and as far as I could see, it looked as if I were sitting on a furrow of a plowed field. Must have been some small tremor in the ocean bottom east of me. I was unable to tell the height of the waves when I first saw them, but I was greatly relieved to find that they were not of a size to cause concern.

There are still a lot of things floating around the cabin. We could have used more time for stowing gear and making more shelving. All the gear is stowed where I want it except for the last two or three carts full that we put aboard in the early morning hours of departure day.

I look forward to the taping sessions every evening. It gives me mental release from the thoughts that whiz around my brain. I get a strange feeling from talking to the air, but I realize there will be a point to it all when I get in and that it really isn't lunacy. I've already changed the radio and RDF batteries. I play the radio during most of my waking hours. I need the sound for a feeling of companionship—confirmation that mankind has not ceased to exist around me. It helps reassure me that I am not the last human being on earth. If this feeling took over, it would probably be the most terrifying experience for me on the journey.

Today I have really begun to enjoy the trip—not trying to do too much in a day—just keeping abreast slowly. Time seems to go by quicker now. I find the trip thus far much as I envisioned it when I read of other undertakings like this.

Getting around Hatteras is now my major topic of concentration. Storm petrels appeared late this evening—an omen of weather to come.

Fran's Log:
The TV weather map looked a lot better tonight in what I think is your neighborhood.

I've been hoping for news about the Singlehanded Transatlantic Race, but there has been no report about it so far.

I love you and I miss you, but I don't wish for you to be back here so much as I wish I were with you sharing whatever there is. I'm feeling fine. I'm sleeping well, and I'm unwinding a little. In my anxious moments about you I just would like to hear that you're all right and that nothing seems unmanageable. Please be having a good time and being happy.

DAY 4: *SUNDAY, JUNE 13*

Log:
Northeaster all day. Gulf Stream really rough. At least 12-foot waves. Force 5 wind. I put in the first set of reef points. Quite a job. I'm very tired. Will try to sleep in quarter berth tonight. Boat a little wet inside but not bad considering what we went through. Fine boat.

Tape:
2100. We have a very strong easterly wind, high waves, and confused seas. *Folly* is performing beautifully, and Jake is handling it well. Compass heading 40°. No rain. Overcast and muggy.

When I went up to reef the main, in order to avoid being
pitched off the boat, I wrapped my knees around the mast. After
the reefing points were set, I noticed blood covering my hand,
but I had felt no pain. I discovered when I got back to the
cockpit that I had gouged my thumb on a halyard in a very
sensitive area, but because of the excitement of the moment, I
felt nothing. Reefing took a great deal of energy, but I have a
great feeling of accomplishment after my first bout of sail-han-
dling in a fairly dangerous situation.

There were two other minor casualties during my love affair
with the mast. I bruised the right side of my chest on one of the
halyard winches and mangled a Swisher Sweet cigar in the top
pocket of my foul weather pants. I lovingly repaired the cigar
and smoked it as a reward when I returned to the cockpit.

Conditions are highly unfavorable for sleeping tonight. I have
to keep a constant check on all the gear, as this is the first time
Folly and I have ridden out really rough conditions singlehanded.

Six hours' sleep in the past twenty-four hours. I am convinced
that rest, food, and keeping dry will be my prime considerations.
Up to now I've been making headway on my rest. I've moved
loose gear out of the quarter berth and rolled out my sleeping
bag for a rough-weather sleeping place.

I'm at a standoff with food. I still haven't cooked a hot meal,
but I'm working my way through the fresh food supplies. After
reefing the main and smoking my cigar, I went below and got
two apples. Since I'm not a fresh fruit lover on land, I was
surprised to find that they were the best-tasting apples I had had
since I was a kid—sweet and juicy. Earlier in the day I ate four
bananas. I am bravely continuing my race between nutrition
and rot, but at any moment I could grow a tail and start swinging through the cabin. I'm looking forward to opening a jar of
peanut butter, and I have some boiled eggs in ready reserve, but
I have found that peeling a boiled egg over a trash container on
a tossing boat is a real challenge in acrobatics. I spend a lot of
time peeling while suspended in midair.

I am acutely aware of how much energy it takes to do deck
work and get about the boat, but I am feeling in better shape
physically than I have in a long time—like a teenager again. I am

very pleased with the efficiency with which I accomplish tasks on deck. No wasted effort, and all my mental planning and preparation are really paying off. My preparation of deck gear is good in rough weather. It's easy to handle.

An awareness of not having someone here to pick me up if I fall overboard is always on my mind. A great deal more care is necessary than when sailing with others aboard. My first major mistake here could be my last. Today I felt was my initiation day for foul weather, and so far I have done well. I'm very pleased to find that I can remain relaxed for the most part in rough weather and not be gripped with fear. Perhaps I should be at times, but I'm not.

I'm very proud of the boat's performance. The Atlantis foul weather gear is working beautifully, too. Only my face and beard take the abuse of dunkings, and I am quickly learning to be comfortable with small deposits of salt in my beard.

I am plagued by leaks. There are a couple of deck leaks, and the companionway hatch cover leaks from the backside. All the weather reports from land say "clear and beautiful." Wish the reporter were sitting here with me.

The sounds of waves breaking over the boat and gear rattling around prompted me to seek out a hard rock AM music station and turn up the volume. (Note: This was the first phase of a minor addiction to rock and roll that I was to develop during this passage.) My tastes usually run along symphonic lines, but I have to admit that good solid rock at a very high decibel level transfers the anxieties one feels locked in a small boat in the middle of a gale to the anxieties of organized sound made by man rather than nature.

I'm beginning to use the first of my six hundred cigars from Waycross. And I'm just about to finish the second gallon of water carried above my regular supply. My big treat of the day while taping now is a bag of M&M candies.

No sextant shot today. Now that it's dark I can see a star or two between the clouds. The barometer is rising. I'm enjoying the experience of sailing the Gulf Stream. It will prepare me for the North Atlantic. After I work my way around Hatteras, I will be relieved because the coast of the U.S. will drop away to the west. I am now a little northwest of where I had planned to be at this stage of the trip.

Fran's Log:

I've decided I'll feel better if I pay no attention to the weather map. Tonight it shows small patches of clear weather offshore surrounded by large blobs of murky weather, and I don't know whether you're in a patch or a blob.

There was a story in the news about a whale. I wonder if you've seen any whales yet.

DAY 5: *MONDAY, JUNE 14*

Log:

Noon position (1700) 34°20′N, 75°20′W. Fuel 17.5 gallons (ran engine 10 minutes today). Water 60 (used 1 gallon; discovered another under hatch).

Tape:

2000. A hurricane hunter with a big pancake on top circled overhead and blew a horn at me this morning. I waved to him from the companionway. Maybe he will report my position, and you will hear. My first contact with another human being gave me a genuinely warm feeling. That was the longest I had ever been without knowing that someone else knew definitely that I was alive and well.

I've eaten more today. Milk with Ovaltine for breakfast. A peanut butter sandwich—double decker—and Vienna sausage tonight. I made a quart of lemonade trying to save the lemons. Two had gone bad on one end. I finished the bananas. Hurrah! Tonight for dinner I had biscuits, boiled egg, Vienna sausage, and the rest of the lemonade. I'm using the heat of the day as an excuse for not lighting the stove.

We are busting along now. I took down the working jib and put up the 150 percent genny. Hope I will have good sense to know when to take it down. Wave action is still rough but it's rather moderate compared to the past twenty-four hours. *Folly* is performing superbly.

I used three long straps of velcro to lash the working jib down on deck behind the netting that covers the lifelines. Then I cut sail ties about three feet long and put them on the handrails outside the companionway. I'll secure the working jib with these next time I go on the foredeck. Keeping one sail stowed on deck while the other flies gives me more room in the cabin.

My sextant shots were good today. Three shots confirm that I am rounding Hatteras, and my dead reckoning and sextant shots are very close.

And today I saw my whales. When I first sighted them coming at the boat, I thought they might be killer whales, but they were playful pilot whales. They were in a pod of twenty to thirty, and they came very close to the boat. They were with me for a good hour and a half. I sat quietly at the helm and just sailed with them. They really took my breath away.

Tonight the stars are so bright I wonder if you're seeing the same stars, baby, and I feel very close to you.

I ran the engine for ten minutes today just before the whales appeared. The ignition key wanted to stick in the ignition switch. I first noticed this tendency after Jake and Bill messed up the cockpit with king mackerel blood on my trial run offshore and threw buckets of salt water over the cockpit—and the ignition switch—to clean it up.

I dried out wet gear in the warm sun today. I'm surprised at how well things wet with salt water have dried.

I've noticed the first gear wear. The piece of shock cord tied into the topping lift to prevent chafing on the leech of the mainsail tore loose. That's on the top of my list for attention in the morning. My day's work went much faster today. I'm looking forward to a good night's rest.

Fran's Log: I woke up this morning thinking, "OK, this nonsense has gone on long enough. It's time for him to come home now." But I don't really want you to. I want you to be out there enjoying sailing.

The weather map still provides a puzzlement every night. It looks as if the trough of the old low-pressure system is lying right along your course. You could be having winds dead on your nose, or you could be sitting in one of those voice-of-doom low centers, or you could be having good winds and good sailing. It's useless to speculate, but I do it anyway. Tonight we're decidely northeasterish here, but the moon is beautiful. I hope you're seeing it, too.

DAY 6: *TUESDAY, JUNE 15*

Log:

Noon position 36°40′N, 72°30′W.

Tape:

0945. I'm eating an apple. At 0830 I came out of the cabin drinking a can of grapefruit juice and enjoying the beautiful morning. Looked toward the bow. There was a damp, limp velcro strip hanging where the working jib had been lashed. The jib was gone. I made my way forward, examining the edge of the boat and all the deck area. I couldn't believe my eyes until I actually stood where the jib had been. The very first thought in my mind was that this headsail did not carry a sail number, so if, by some strange twist of events, it were found, no one would be concerned about me.

I sat down in the cockpit and thought carefully about my options. I now had a storm jib and a 150 percent genoa. We had hoped to be able to get a little more headsail inventory, but it was financially impossible. All the sails were in fine shape when I left, but I hadn't expected to lose one over the side—especially the working jib.

The solution was clear. I promised you if anything upped the odds a great deal against my success, I would come into the nearest safe port. As you've often said, I'm not out here to prove anything to anyone, and this is no place to practice unnecessary heroics. If I continued and got to England successfully with a 150 percent genoa and no means of reefing it, you would have every reason not to support me in any other adventure.

When I saw the jib gone, my heart didn't drop, and I had no trouble deciding what to do. Dad and Mom will be happy to know that I had the good sense to come back. And I know you won't be disappointed in me. It has been an experience worth having, and I know you'll be glad I had it. I said if I got out of the jetties, I'd be happy, and I did that. The reporters might not understand coming back because of the loss of a jib. And it will be too late in the season to make another start. Malvina can keep that half dollar, and I'll keep mine. That half dollar will mean a lot to me.

With a decision to turn around firmly set in my mind, I turned my attention to the question of where to go. I was about 180 miles east of Cape Henry, and if I turned west and headed directly for Cape Henry, it would take approximately two days, and the last twenty-four hours I would have Cape Hatteras south of me. The most severe conditions around Cape Hatteras occur in a northeaster, and I have already experienced fairly heavy northeast winds on this trip. Just north of Cape Hatteras is not where I want to be in such conditions, especially without a working jib.

On a rhumb line, Charleston is approximately 480 nautical miles from my position. As I work my way around Hatteras, I'll be working directly against the pull of the Gulf Stream, and this could cut my progress in half. The sailing directions warn not to enter ports south of Cape Hatteras without local knowledge until reaching Charleston, which has an excellent entrance. After reading the sailing directions and pulling out a large-scale chart that takes me from north of Cape Hatteras to Charleston, I turned *Folly* on a course toward Charleston. The chart doesn't give great detail for entrances into port, but I hope that after rounding Hatteras, I can close land and maybe get local knowledge from fishermen or someone to come in earlier than Charleston.

I made my decision and changed course less than an hour ago. Can't cross the Atlantic without a working jib. That scratches the trip. I've qualified for the Singlehanded Transatlantic Race, but I've also learned a lot about myself, and I'm not going to talk singlehanding any more. I promise that any project I do is going to be with you. I don't want to do any alone. We have a well-equipped boat, and I don't mind paying for it. *Folly* looks good. She'll take you about anywhere you want to go if you handle her right—and don't do anything dumb like leave the jib lashed with velcro.

It's going to be a long journey back, but maybe I'll get to read a book. I'll have to stay up and watch for shipping as I get closer. I mustn't get in trouble close to land. I'm working my way west for about fifty-seven miles, and then I'll try to head south. It may be a little tricky with the wind blowing the way it is. I'll just be very careful and get us back in one piece.

Forty years old. A man has to find himself, and I have. Everything's going to be fine. I'd love to get to England, but the only way I'll get there now is to fly. I won't do it singlehanded. Not without you. And certainly not around the world.

2100. In good spirits. Here we are busting along, ninety-to-nothing, averaging a 30-degree heel. Winds are slightly overpowering for the genny, but I think the rigging is strong enough so that it will hold and the genny would blow out first. Boy, I am happy that we added the material to the foot. Water comes up in the bottom of the sail. We're heading due south after coming fifty-seven miles back in. We're slightly north of Hatteras. A 180-degree heading is the best I can get, but we are making good time.

I knew when I came out of the Gulf Stream heading west—a line from deep blue to pale blue. I'd never seen the edge of it before, and there it was.

Having seen the ocean out here, nature is now of a magnitude to me that supersedes physical science as we know it. I feel like a real part of nature—more so than when I spent time in the woods. It's a feeling of being a part of something really great—the universe. It's a humbling thing to be out on the ocean and know that it has the power to squash you in a minute with no effort at all. Like a man slapping a fly. The fact that it doesn't moment after moment is awe-inspiring. Being with others breeds confidence because you feel one can protect the other.

I feel as if I'm talking ninety-to-nothing and not saying much. I just don't want to forget any of the sensations I've had out here.

The cabin is still a mess. I'll try to clean up a little when I get back in. We have a lot of everything aboard—best-equipped boat in Fernandina. How many men do you know with cigars for two months in advance? And bottom paint for two jobs? You and I can motor down the waterway to get *Folly* back home.

Waves are breaking over the bow now, but I think everything is all right. For me this project hasn't been a failure at all. It's a smashing success. I would do it all again.

In my dreams I'm still collecting nuts and bolts, drilling in the right places, and trying not to forget anything, but the only thing I left behind that I really need is you.

There is a star I can barely see out the hatch.

Fran's Log:
I can only think of your enjoying the boat and the sea.

DAY 7: *WEDNESDAY, JUNE 16*

Log:
> 1300   Put chafing gear on genny sheet. Seas fairly calm. Reading *Alice in Wonderland.*

Tape:
2000. I'm getting Nag's Head, North Carolina, on the radio. We're sailing about 250°, and the boat's been screaming along. The weather and water are beautiful. The barometer is holding pretty well at 30.20. As I move south, it will probably drop just a little because the pressure around Fernandina is about 30.10. The heel indicator is registering between 20 and 30 degrees. Inside the cabin I don't feel it too much as my bunk is on the down side, but doing anything takes a bit of effort because of the heel.

I'm going at navigation like I've been doing it for years. I'll close land to verify my position.

The rigging might have stretched. Herb Piker said it would stretch a little. *Folly's* never been out in conditions like this. This boat will be worth a million dollars, knowing what she'll do.

I'm not eating a lot, but I don't think I've lost too much weight. I still don't have the courage to look at myself in the mirror. Today I ate a double-decker peanut butter sandwich and half a quart of Ovaltine. I ate a can of asparagus and enjoyed that. I still don't miss ice. I've also had a can or two of fruit juice, and I discovered another apple.

There are more than a hundred men and women on the ocean singlehanding from England. I wish them well. Hope none of them has lost a sail. Hope they are all in good shape and eating well. Today I'm thinking I might want to singlehand short races.

It will be nice to walk with you on the beach again and hold your hand.

Fran's Log:
There was a news report on the Transatlantic Race tonight. There are 125 on their way, including the big one, and they have had bad weather.

I miss you. I felt worried this afternoon and just wanted word that everything was all right. I love you.

DAY 8: *THURSDAY, JUNE 17*

Log:
Rough night. Had to put in hatch board at 0200. Some water in cabin. Log registering too low.

Tape:
2100. Good spirits. I don't know that I've felt any better physically in a long time. I feel rested. I even felt so good I washed the dishes.

We had a rough night last night. We were screaming along and water was coming in. Broke a turning block on the starboard side. I replaced the block this morning and it's doing fine. We'll see how the one I put on does. If it pops, I have four more.

It's cozy in here with the lamp. I've brought the tiller lines inside the cabin to make fine adjustments to course from inside. I'll read more *Alice in Wonderland* tonight. I listened to a Charleston radio station today and was comforted to know I was heading south. Charleston has been having rain, but we haven't had rain out here. There's a red sunset tonight. Red sky at night, sailor's delight.

Tomorrow night I'll have to stay awake closing land. I saw a ship west of me tonight heading south. I see a ship going north now. I'm close to the shipping lanes. I have the curtains drawn so the cabin lights will show outside. I can see the cloud cover over land.

DAY 9: *FRIDAY, JUNE 18*

Log:

Spent 8 gallons of gas trying to find a place to come in. No luck. Can't do that again. Wasted a whole day. Will I ever get in?

Tape:

0400. Strange thing just happened. I woke up about 0305 without the alarm. The main was slapping around. We were becalmed. I looked over the stern and saw a light flashing. It was Cape Lookout. I wasn't sure I would see that lighthouse. If the wind hadn't dropped, I would never have seen it. Boy, did that feel good. That's the first visual reference I've had in over a week. We're about eighty miles from Cape Fear. I am laying a course to Cape Fear.

Fran's Log:

This morning I got the tag end of the weather report on the "Today Show," and the newsman was saying, "And that's good news for the Bermuda Race." Well, if it's good news for the Bermuda Race, it's good news for you because you ought to be getting up toward that part of the ocean now. My conservative markings on the chart put you somewhere off Hatteras, but you could be farther along than that.

DAY 10: *SATURDAY, JUNE 19*

Tape:

2000. A Coast Guard plane just flew over. I guess I scared the hell out of people on the beach. I went in to about two miles off shore. Part of the morning and into the afternoon I tried to stop deep-sea fishermen to get local knowledge for getting into the Cape Fear area. Waved lifejackets, blew the horn. But as I would approach a boat, it would run off. I guess I just looked too good sailing, and they were afraid I would tangle their fishing gear. I'm beginning to feel like the Ancient Mariner.

"Wearing" is the word for it. I'll have to work my way down to Charleston. I'm about 150 miles from there including rounding Frying Pan Shoals. The weather is supposed to get bad. I hate to sound discouraged, but I've been slopping around out here. I feel as if I've been trying to work my way south for so long. Well, I saw a little bit of the North Carolina coast.

DAY 11: *SUNDAY, JUNE 20*

Log:

0745 position 32°50′N, 78°40′W.

Very high seas. Two rainstorms last night. Will hold this tack for 55 miles from reset of log.

I'm catching hell from weather now. Charleston tomorrow night. *Maybe!*

Recollection:

On the last two days at sea I was too busy to tape. Early in the morning I picked up the light at the end of Frying Pan Shoals. I was northeast of it and working my way around it. Winds were high and seas were running very high. About 1030 I dropped the genny and set the storm jib. As soon as I had it up, I looked up off the bow, and there was a large black freighter that had turned around and was approaching me. I hove to—which the storm jib did very nicely—and I talked with the captain of the *Boston* over the power hailer. He asked me if I was in difficulty, and I explained to him that I would like assistance entering a port, possibly from the Coast Guard. He said no because I still had sail. I had to agree with him but could not make him understand that in high winds I could blow the genny out, and I was very worried about trying to make my way in under storm jib—that, coupled with the fact that the sailing directions warned against entering ports along this coast without local knowledge.

I could see the tower at the end of Frying Pan Shoals off on the horizon to starboard. The captain kindly made an effort to verify our position, but I couldn't hear him. I thanked him. I was very comforted to have spoken to him. It was the first time a large ship had ever turned around to speak to me, and the men aboard her will never know how grateful I was.

After the *Boston* left my vicinity, I tried working to windward with the storm jib and did not find it efficient at all. I hoisted the genny again, sailed into the southbound shipping lane, and allowed three ships to pass me so that I could be spotted and they would know I was all right. I was now making my way across Long Bay and had decided to continue on to Charleston. My next landfall would be Cape Romain.

The weather continued to deteriorate. During the evening we were hit by severe squalls, and the boat was heeled in excess of 40 degrees as we worked to windward. Water poured over the coaming into the cockpit. I was at the tiller and was gripped with an urge to do everything in my power to help *Folly* work to windward. An empty plastic gallon milk jug was floating in the cockpit. I picked it up, cut the bottom off, and proceeded to bail. Although my efforts were futile so far as helping *Folly* a great deal, they satisfied me psychologically because I felt more involved in the struggle between the sea, the bad weather, and the boat.

When Jake could handle the wind and it was not so gusty, I would go below for shelter from the weather. At 0300 I was sitting on the corner of the sink next to the companionway, wearing only my shorts, stuffing a towel in the back of the leaking companionway hatch. I reached for the grab rail overhead, inadvertently releasing my right hand from the hatch before grasping the rail. At that instant the boat fell off a fair-sized wave. In what seemed to be slow motion, I was thrown, with my back almost touching the top of the cabin, across the dinette. I crashed with my right elbow and the entire length of my body against the starboard portlights and fell straight down onto the starboard cushioned seat behind the dinette. While flying across the cabin I felt like Captain Marvel or Superman, and it seemed to take a very long time to reach those windows. Fortunately I didn't break a bone and only received a few bruises. My right elbow turned black but caused no problems.

All evening I stayed west of the shipping lane and catnapped for no more than ten- or fifteen-minute stretches. Food for the day was minimal. A Vienna sausage sandwich at midday was the heaviest thing I ate.

Fran's Log:

I don't mean I would say no if you really want to do a round-the-world trip, but I'd rather do it with you. If I could have word right this minute that everything is OK, I would be perfectly happy.

DAY 12: *MONDAY, JUNE 21*

Log:

0600 Water green. Going south.
2100 Stormy weather. Tried to get into Charleston. Dragged the bottom. What a harrowing experience. Dead tired. Will try to sleep a little.

Recollection:

Dawn of the twenty-first found me coming into the area of Cape Romain. I was tired after a night of bad weather. I had not been able to pick up the light at Cape Romain, where a barge and tugboat were waiting to go in at the entrance.

The sailing directions say that in bad weather storms make up over the cape and visibility could be nil and that no attempt should be made to enter the port then. These were the conditions existing that morning. I could not see land because of bad weather.

I set a course from the tug to run along the coast and find the first of three offshore buoys that led to Charleston. At this point I noticed an eighteen-inch tear in the genny just above the foot of the sail where the turnbuckle from the lifeline wore on it. The turnbuckle had been heavily taped, but in the severe weather the tape had worn through. I moved the turning block up on its track toward the bow and increased the pressure on the leech of the sail, taking some of the strain off the foot. I took out my sail repair kit—which contained no spare material—and went forward. I attempted to dry off the sail and tape the rip with sail tape. It would not hold because the surface couldn't be kept dry. Very little pressure was being exerted on the torn area so I left it alone and hoped that a Hood sail was all I had heard it was. It was.

I found the first and second buoys and was making for the third, hoping to close it around sunset. As luck would have it, thunderstorms were approaching. I was so close to Charleston that I felt I could motor the rest of the way in a lot more comfortably than trying to sail in so I turned on the iron man and went forward to drop the genny.

All of a sudden a new and fascinating sound emerged from the engine room. The starter had reengaged for some reason. I ran back to the cockpit and shut the engine down. After two or three minutes, I restarted the engine, and all seemed well. I went forward to take down the genny a second time. I had it down on deck when the starter reengaged again. I went back to the cockpit, turned off the ignition switch, and went back to the bow to rehoist the genny. To my amazement, the starter began running again, trying to start the engine without the ignition key on.

I went back to the cockpit, reached inside the cabin, and shut off the master switch. I could smell odors of an electrical short and quickly jumped into the cabin and pulled the steps out to look at the engine. It was in order. The short had to be in the ignition switch, which had given me forewarning that a problem was building. I reached out and touched the ignition key. It was hot as blazes. The short was severe. I examined for fire and found none.

By this time it was beginning to get dark, and we were being hit by another thunderstorm. I put the steps back in place and got sail on again. Visibility was very poor. I thought I could see a white light blinking south of me in the distance, and I headed for it. It was dark and raining heavily.

The next few minutes were the most harrowing I had ever spent with *Folly*. She touched bottom and heeled over. I thought surely I had run onto the north side of the jetties. When her keel hit the bottom because of waves running fairly high, it would jar every bone in my body. In the gusting winds, she would heel over and be free for a second or two, and when the wind let up, she would touch again; but I managed to work her around, little by little, until we were headed due east. She worked her way forward, and quite suddenly, as though sliding off a shelf, we found ourselves in deep water again.

I decided not to attempt to get in tonight and thought I might possibly sail on to Fernandina. We had suffered no damage except that a variety of items had been thrown all over the cabin, and everything was in even more disarray than it had been before. I was thoroughly exhausted but very thankful that the engine had acted up when it had. If the engine had worked, I would have driven the boat hard aground and would have been unable to get her off. It was only the strong gusts of wind hitting the sails and causing severe heeling that allowed us to work our way free.

At about 2200 I could see ships coming in to the Charleston sea buoy, and the Charleston lighthouse was visible along with light from land, as the stormy weather had abated. I headed due east to get well away from shipping traffic. I looked down in the cabin and was appalled at the chaos below. I said aloud that there was no reason to live like a wild animal. For the next five hours I rearranged the cabin in a disposition bordering on rage.

DAY 13: *TUESDAY, JUNE 22*

At 0300 I set a southerly course and knew that I had to get a little rest or I would fly apart at the seams. I lay down across the dinette seat and slept soundly for all of thirty minutes. After waking, I stuck my head out the hatch, and there was the Charleston light flashing away. I decided then to go back to make the entrance by sunrise.

I ate a sandwich and was now ready to have another try at going in. The weather was very cooperative. I was approaching the entrance along with some heavy shipping traffic, and I passed close to a shrimping fleet coming out of Charleston. I followed, in a manner of speaking, a large freighter going in and had a gorgeous sail through the entrance, past Fort Sumter, and on into the Ashley River on the south side of the Battery.

After I cleared the jetties and got into the harbor, a large Coast Guard workboat passed, and we waved to each other. As I got into the Ashley River, an Army Corps of Engineers launch passed close by. I hailed them. I asked if they could call and ask the Coast Guard to give me assistance getting into the Municipal Marina, which is protected by a large concrete wall. After talking to the Coast Guard on the radio, they said that I should just drop my anchor outside the entrance to the marina and someone from the marina would eventually tow me in. I had set up the anchor and line and all docklines while coming in through the jetties so I was prepared for whatever maneuver was necessary.

We were within a hundred yards of the Municipal Marina when one of the men on the Army Corps of Engineers launch asked if I could use a hand. I answered that I sure could. The launch motored up alongside me and Brian Bialsford came aboard. He was from Massachusetts and was also an experienced sailor. He was quite familiar with the marina so I gave him the helm, and I handled the sails. We sailed into the marina and up to the north side of the fuel dock, dropped all sail, and threw the docklines to eager hands on the dock.

It seemed like a very nonchalant ending to a great twelve-day adventure.

PART 3

Here We Go Again

6

Preparation: The Second Time Around

On June 22 Ed called me from Charleston. He was exhausted, and he was disappointed that he had not made it all the way to England. But after 1,182 miles of singlehanding, he was pleased with himself and with *Folly*. He had seen whales—and the beauty and power and mystery of the sea. He had wanted to touch Stonehenge—something old—and after this voyage he said, "I've touched something a lot older than Stonehenge." It had been a real adventure, but he did not immediately talk of trying again.

In Charleston we began the cleanup campaign. *Folly* had taken on several gallons of water. We threw away the soggy red shag carpet—at last. Then we bailed out the under-seat lockers. Fortunately, most of the things stored there were canned goods, heavily coated with lanolin, and dry food that had been given extra protection in plastic bags. We spread everything out to dry in the cockpit and on the dock.

We bought a new ignition switch to replace the one that had corroded out after its constant saltwater bath, and Ed mended the rip that had begun in the overworked genny. He cut a patch from the sailbag for the repair, as the spare sailcloth we had pleaded for had arrived in Atlanta the day after Ed's departure from Fernandina.

Except for missing a working jib, *Folly* was now in good shape again, and the trip down the Intracoastal Waterway to Fernandina—a familiar one—was fun as well as beautiful.

Both in Charleston and back in Fernandina friends and reporters unanimously asked the question. "Will you try again?"

In Charleston the answer was, "I don't know." Ed didn't want to commit himself until he had achieved some distance from the strain of the first attempt. We didn't discuss it. If he wanted to do it, I wanted him to. At the age of eighty he will not turn to me and say, "If it hadn't been for you . . ." If he didn't want to do it, there were a lot of voyages we could make together.

As he talked about his trip, I could see that he was more than ever convinced that both he and *Folly* were capable of the Atlantic crossing. He still wanted to do it, and now deep down he knew that he could—the two basic reasons for setting sail in the first place, raised to the next power. When he told me that he had decided to go again the next June, it was no surprise. I had a fleeting memory of the way I had felt at 4:00 A.M. on June 10, thought, "Some people never learn," and pulled out my yellow pad again.

But there were two major differences. This time my list would be considerably shorter. And this time we knew what we were doing. It would be a slightly more relaxed year. Sam was aging fast. To save his energy and ours, not to mention our pocketbooks, we decided to limit our trips south to every third weekend. We could begin getting *Folly* ready for another voyage, and the pace should be moderate enough to allow us to go sailing occasionally.

Our first concern, obviously, centered on our sail inventory.

We ordered a 130 percent genoa from Gilreath Sails in Atlanta and asked that they check all the stitching on our old sails and put a more substantial patch on the larger genny. From Mr. Poulsen at Eastern Shore Sails in Alabama we ordered a working jib and a zippered acrylic tube bag for storing sails on deck— to provide secure storage and free some space below.

Ranking right up there with adequate sails was the problem of keeping the cabin, and more specifically Ed's bunk, dry. The wild ride back into Charleston had revealed deck leaks. It had also revealed the need for a cover—or turtle—over our sliding companionway hatch to deflect the flow of water finding its way below when waves were rolling over the deck. The sprinkles coming through the deck leaks and the cupfuls coming in under the hatch were not life-threatening. They just reduced life in the cabin to soggy misery, and just below "sails" on Ed's list of priorities this time was the word "comfort."

We spent one of our weekends at Fernandina forcing water into *Folly* and trying to figure out where it was coming in. We found one hole. We had asked the yard to repair a split in our teak toe rail. They had repaired the split, but in the process they had drilled one pin-sized hole in the wrong place and had forgotten to fill it up with something. Ed plugged it and discovered that he had slowed the incoming water considerably. On general principles we lifted a decorative strip of teak on deck and ran a generous bead of silicone sealer under it before putting it down again. We were gaining on the problem.

For the turtle we shamelessly went back to Jake Mottayaw, who foolishly was still speaking to us. He and Ed designed a turtle under which the hatch would slide. Jake built it of oak and half-inch marine plywood and sent it home to Atlanta with us for painting. With his characteristic genius he had produced a cover that fitted its limited space and fulfilled its function—or appeared to, anyway. The test would come later.

As an added precaution Ed drilled small, almost unnoticeable holes at the bottoms of the under-seat lockers so that if water still came in, it would drain onto the cabin sole and into the bilge.

At one point early in our renewed preparations, we were reading in bed late one night—a shared addiction. I read that Queen Elizabeth II of England would be celebrating her Silver Jubilee during 1977. I mentioned the fact to Ed. He was delighted and immediately decided to dedicate his voyage to her.

A week or two later he had settled on a gift—fifty Bicentennial silver dollars, one representing each state of the Union—or two for each year of Her Majesty's reign. It would be a gift from the people of the United States to the Queen.

Jack Mason, a fine potter who taught in the Art Department

The presentation of a Proclamation for Queen Elizabeth II and a Certificate appointing Ed Lormand Admiral of the Georgia Navy, June 1, 1977. Left to right, Secretary of State of Georgia, Ben W. Fortson Jr.; Fran; Ed, and Norman Underwood, Executive Secretary to Govenor George Busbee.

at the college, made and donated a beautiful vase with a lid. Our neighborhood banker at the Citizens and Southern Bank gathered together the silver dollars. Ed and I lined the vase with velvet and had a small silver plate engraved, "To Queen Elizabeth II for Her Silver Jubilee 1977 from the People of the United States of America." She would receive many fine gifts during the year, but it was unlikely that many would be delivered in such an exotic way, and we knew that none would bring with them more sincere good wishes.

We were generally better organized than the year before because we had time and because we had learned a lot on the first voyage. We reduced our estimate of quantities of alcohol and kerosene that would be needed. During the year we dipped into Ed's supply when we were aboard, and we didn't replenish. We thought that he would still have more than enough for a crossing of any reasonable length.

My food lists were similar to the previous year's with a few changes. I reduced the amount of staples such as flour and cornmeal and yeast, doubting that Ed would try any extensive baking. And this time, instead of buying cases of single-serving soups and stews, I watched grocery store specials during the year and bought regular-sized cans at a considerable saving. If Ed didn't want a whole can of beans, the leftovers would keep at least a day.

In provisioning food I used the "dirty trick" method. Canned chili, tamales, and chow mein are among Ed's all-time favorite foods, along with several other such canned delicacies. I suspected that if the supply of any one of these were large enough, he would eat it every night until the supply thinned enough to be alarming. Therefore I put aboard only three to six cans of each of the favorites, forcing him into a varied diet.

This time we varnished the cans instead of coating them with anhydrous lanolin. We were able to work faster, and this time Ed did most of the work himself. Aside from getting the job done, he was able to see for himself what he was taking. When the food was put aboard the boat, Ed put everything away himself while I noted locations on the list and the chart he would have with him. He divided the food so that he had half of it— some of everything—in one set of lockers easily accessible on the starboard side and the other half in less handy places under the port bunk. After the halfway point he could start on the second half of the food supply. This forced still more variety.

The eggs dipped in boiling water and then coated with vaseline had lasted for a surprisingly long time. Again we went through the egg routine, but this time we did not coat the hard-boiled eggs. On the first voyage those so treated had spoiled before the uncooked ones.

For fresh fruit and vegetables we begged plastic milk crates from the grocery store. Citrus fruits were wrapped individually in aluminum foil and placed in a crate lashed down in the forward cabin. All other fresh fruits and vegetables were placed in a crate lashed on deck with a white fabric cover fitted over the top. The crates had holes on the bottom and sides. No effort was made to protect the contents from salt water. The cover would protect them from the sun. This was one of many lessons we had learned as a result of loitering around the dock talking to transient voyagers. The fresh food thus stored would eventually shrivel and dry, but it would still be edible and would not rot.

I made a clothes list and packed one bag of cold-weather clothes and one bag of warm-weather clothes and indicated to Ed which was which. And once more Peggy Wilson gathered up twelve boxes of Swisher Sweets cigars and sent them to the beach. I went through the medical kit, replaced everything whose expiration date had passed and asked the pharmacist about the possible effect of age or temperature extremes on our supply of prescription drugs. It was a relief to our budget when he said that everything was still usable.

Our financial situation was still tight. Ed was not teaching the night class this year. On the other hand, we were not traveling quite so much, and except for sails and renewing our insurance, most of our major expenses had already been taken care of. Our new insurance premium was a pleasant surprise. It hadn't gone up. It seemed to be the only thing that hadn't. We were constantly appalled at the rate at which prices had increased in twelve months. To help the ready cash supply, I went to work for a temporary secretarial agency and worked two or three days a week from January through May. The extra money helped at the moment even if we didn't clear much after taxes. And Commander Smith at the Mayflower Marina in Plymouth kindly agreed to hold our reservation for the following July with no additional deposit. We sometimes felt as if we were in the middle of a slow-motion, not-very-instant replay.

That feeling evaporated around the end of April. From then on nothing was slow-motion, and we were definitely covering new territory. We discovered that we couldn't get to Graham's for haulout, bottom-painting, changing through-hull fittings, and adding running backstays. The Main Street Bridge in Jacksonville was down and could not be opened for boat traffic. The current prediction was that the bridge would be down until midwinter. We had to have the Main Street Bridge opened to get to Graham's, and midwinter was too late for Ed's projected June departure.

After telephoning everyone in town who had a sailboat, we finally settled on a boatyard at Jacksonville Beach as a possible alternative—if they could take us on such short notice. When Ed came home, he called the manager. He agreed to work us into their schedule for all the work except the running backstays. We could take *Folly* down on Saturday, May 14, and pick her up to return to Fernandina on May 22. We were relieved to be able to meet our schedule, and we decided that Fate didn't intend for us to have running backstays.

On Friday, May 13 (I should have anticipated disaster), we went through our Keystone Cops car-jockeying routine, and Saturday morning we motor-sailed *Folly* down to Jacksonville Beach. We checked in with the manager of the yard, went out for a good seafood dinner, and slept aboard *Folly*.

The next Friday, for the return maneuvers, Grady and Marceil Wildes, friends from Waycross, came with us to reclaim *Folly* and start north up the Waterway. As soon as we went aboard, we noticed a little water under the table. We had stacked things there to get them out of the way of workmen who would change the through-hull fittings. Now the area looked as though somebody had left a hatch open and it had rained in—or somebody had been careless with a hose on the dock.

We hurriedly got underway so that the outgoing tide wouldn't strand us in the boatyard. Ed had several projects he wanted to do on the way back to Fernandina.

Ed reached into a locker for something. Water. Salt water. Then he looked into the next locker. More water. (This was before he drilled the drain holes.) He pulled out drawers. There was no water standing in them, but the contents had been soaked and were still wet. I was at the tiller still motoring north up the Waterway toward Fernandina. I really did not grasp the magnitude of the disaster until Ed handed Grady the plastic box containing our engine spares. The box was full of salt water.

We couldn't turn back. We had to get *Folly* back to Fernandina. There was work to do and only two more weekends to do it in. And now we had more work than we had bargained for. Everything in the lower lockers had been wet with salt water. Several of them had already been packed for the voyage. Now everything had to be removed, washed, and dried, and we had to replace everything that had been ruined.

What on earth had happened? We discovered a water line in the forward cabin that ran six to eight inches above the cabin sole. *Folly* had been submerged to that extent. But why? Had she been dropped, doing major damage to the hull? The bilge had been nearly full when we came aboard, but that hadn't been alarming after the work that had been done. All the new through-hull fittings looked good, and she didn't appear to be taking on water anywhere.

The only thing to do was get back to Fernandina, call the yard manager, and ask what had happened. The most alarming thing to us was that nobody had told us anything. Accidents can happen anywhere. We just needed to know what the accident was before Ed set out to cross an ocean alone.

The next most alarming thing was that I would have to make a list of the ruined items, including rusting cans of cleaning supplies, dye markers, stopwatch, spare compass light, and engine spares, and spend the next three weeks scouting for replacements. And there was the expense. We had already paid for the yard work, and we had left the yard with damages equal to about half the bill.

All the way back to Fernandina Ed and Grady bailed water out of lockers and spread soggy equipment around the deck to dry. Ed kept an eye on the bilge and the through-hull fittings.

They seemed to be all right. Our best guess was that *Folly* had been put back in the water with an open valve—or a bad valve. The situation had been corrected but not until an alarming amount of water had found its way inside. But why hadn't someone bothered to mention the fact to us?

After we got back to Dell's, Ed stayed to clean up *Folly* while I took Grady and Marceil back to Jacksonville Beach to pick up their car. At the yard, I asked for the manager. He was out. There was no way to reach him, but I wrote an account of our discovery, pointed out that we had to know what had happened, and indicated that we would have to stop payment on our check until we could determine the extent of the damage.

He called Ed on Monday to get more complete information from us and to tell us that he was thoroughly baffled. He was investigating. Then he called again to give us his report. Apparently the mechanic working on *Folly* had left the through-hull packing gland on the shaft loose. She was put back into the water in his absence, and when he returned, the water was over the cabin sole. He pumped her out, closed up the hole, and told no one.

The yard took full responsibility and adjusted our bill to cover the damaged items, which we agreed to return to them. I spent the three remaining weeks scouting the countryside and writing frantic letters to boat equipment dealers, and by the time Ed left, almost everything had been replaced.

But the weekend after we got *Folly* back to Fernandina, we made another chilling discovery. On the trip home from Jacksonville Beach our eyes had rarely strayed above that waterline in the forward cabin. The next weekend while Ed was working on the boat, he looked at the chronometer mounted on the bulkhead. We had always kept it set on Greenwich Time. Now it showed local time. The four-hour difference had bothered some workman enough so that he had felt compelled to reset it. He had accomplished this by shoving the *hour* hand *back* four hours. The hour hand was no longer quite perpendicular at six o'clock. There was a greasy fingerprint inside the glass over the face.

We removed the chronometer from the bulkhead and took it

home with us. Ed reset it to Greenwich Time. We watched it all week and returned it to Fernandina the next weekend. It seemed to be functioning properly.

There had been no earthly reason for anyone to touch the chronometer. Now in the midst of the nerve-wracking strain of last-minute preparations for departure, there was another uncertainty. What else on the boat had been tampered with? Would there be any more surprises?

Ed had promised the yard manager that I would deliver the damaged goods to the yard as soon as he had set sail. I wouldn't have time until then. On the day before Ed left, the manager called to ask for them. Ed promised again that I would deliver them.

On June 1 at 4:00 P.M. there was a ceremony in the rotunda of the Capitol in Atlanta. Governor George Busbee of Georgia had heard about Ed's plan to sail the Atlantic alone and to dedicate his voyage to Queen Elizabeth in celebration of her Silver Jubilee. Representing the governor, his executive secretary Norman Underwood presented Ed a document giving him the honorary title of admiral in the Georgia Navy. Georgia's secretary of state, Ben W. Fortson, Jr., then gave Ed a hand-lettered, beribboned, and gold-sealed proclamation giving him the privilege of representing the governor and the people of Georgia in carrying greetings and good wishes to Her Majesty the Queen on the occasion of her Silver Jubilee. Assistant Secretary of State Ann Adamson was present for the ceremony, as were Duane Riner, the governor's news secretary, and Beau Cutts, our good friend and a writer for the *Atlanta Constitution.*

It was a fine and touching occasion. The governor was demonstrating a lot of faith in a sailor who had already tried once and failed to reach England.

The last days were hectic but not quite so frenzied as the year before. This time Ed had given himself a full day in Fernandina before sailaway time, now set at 10:00 A.M. June 11. Again family and friends were pressed into service, Beau Cutts performing the vital task of wrapping each bottle in Ed's liquor locker (including three splits and one fifth of champagne for special celebrations) in air-gap plastic. He begged off occasionally to write or call in a story.

On the morning of June 11 the crowd was back on the dock, including friends, relatives, reporters, and sightseers. Little John May was one of them, on hand with his characteristic offer, "What can I do to help?" A misguided pelican had tried a landing on the wind indicator at *Folly*'s masthead. The wind indicator lost. We had bought a replacement but hadn't managed to get Ed or anyone else up the mast to install it. Little John was willing, and within an hour of Ed's departure Jake winched him up. The news from the top was bad. The fitting was so corroded that it would be impossible in the time we had to remove it and put on the new one. Jake let Little John down again.

Friends on other boats—ready for the escort to the sea buoy—were vocally impatient to get underway, but Ed refused to leave this time until everything was in place in the cabin. He was only forty minutes behind schedule when Beau and Bill Cutts cast off the dockline.

My mother and I, aboard Jake's *Anna Maru,* and Ed's family, aboard Tommy's *Libtom III,* followed Ed out. And this time, as it was a Saturday morning, we had even more company.

It was a beautiful day with a sturdy southeast breeze. Southeast this time, not northeast. We couldn't have asked for better weather. *Folly* surged out of Cumberland Sound as if she were impatient to get on with it. Ed waited for the *Anna Maru* to get close enough for a shouted good-bye at the sea buoy, and he was gone again.

PART 4

1977 Voyage

7

More Logs, Tapes, and Recollections

DAY 1: *SATURDAY, JUNE 11*

Log:

Fuel on board 19.8 gallons. Water on board 60 gallons plus 4 gallons in jugs.

1050   Shoved off.

1245   Set log halfway between range markers and sea buoy.

1345   St. Mary's sea buoy; 5.75 knots on log. Off to a good start. Wind southeast force 3. Three boats came to sea buoy. Talked to Fran on Jake's boat.

1700   Set first reef in main.

2000   Lit the lamps and now having beer and French bread. I drank a quart of cold milk about 1400.

2230   Did a turn-around to avoid a large ship southbound. Could hear engines.

Fran's Log:

I was on the porch at 9:00 tonight thinking about you, but the thinking-about-you part has been going on all day. I miss you. I hope everything is all right on the boat. At least it should be

Ed in Folly's *cockpit during the final minutes before departure, June 11, 1977. (*Jacksonville Journal, *Don Ray photo)*

more all right than last time. I just want you to be comfortable
and happy and remember to eat and rest.

We couldn't have asked for better weather here. That was a
lot better than last year, too. According to the weather map on
TV tonight, it looks as if you might have several days of good
weather and fair winds.

DAY 2: *SUNDAY, JUNE 12*

Log:

Noon position 31°48′N, east of Savannah in Gulf
Stream.

Remaining fuel 19 gallons. Water 60 + .

Noon   After 23 hours 15 minutes 130¼ miles on log. Best time
ever. We were becalmed one-half hour during this time.

1800   Large freighter passed quarter mile port side. Must be
crossing northbound shipping lane. Second ship seen
heading south fifteen minutes later.

Tape:

1947. We've been moving along. We're right comfortable—
getting back into the routine of seagoing again.

I haven't felt really too well. I took an Alka Selzer and that
helped some. Beau Cutts left me four quarts of milk. I drank
two, and I'm halfway through the third.

If I can get some blocks of sleep tonight down here in the
bunk, that will be nice. I'm hoping the boat will take care of
herself. I've lit all the lights. It will be good to stay down in the
cabin and sleep. It's too hot during the day to stay down here.

2253. I slept for a couple of hours—two one-hour stretches in
the bunk. First time in the bunk, and that helped.

I was looking in the navigation book a little bit, and I had
blurred vision. That's from fatigue and heat. I'll adapt to the
heat, and the fatigue will be taken care of little by little. By
tomorrow I ought to feel pretty rested and can turn my attention
to better food. Haven't had my champagne yet, but my stomach
just hasn't been in the mood for champagne. I had a can of

grapefruit juice and drank a little water when I got up to keep fluids in me. I'm perspiring a bit, but that's to be expected. It will be getting cooler where I'm going, and I'll get more used to the work.

I saw a devil fish come out of the water as I was leaving Fernandina, and I saw one shark's fin today. He didn't make a pass at the log, but he was out that way. I'm trying to notice those things. People always ask if I saw any sharks. I've seen several types of birds. The water is a deep, deep blue.

Baby, I'm sleepy and not halfway through this tape. I'm going to crawl back into my bunk.

Fran's Log:

I've felt very peculiar today. At first I couldn't figure out why. Then I realized it was because I had slept eight and a half solid hours last night. When I first began waking up this morning, I was thinking, "What's on my list to do today?" I thought yesterday was still in front instead of behind us.

DAY 3: *MONDAY, JUNE 13*

Log:

Noon position 32°42'.8N, 76°2'W. Day's run 132¾. Remaining fuel 19 gallons. Water 60 + .

Tape:

This is really June 14. It's after midnight.

We slowed down today. Down to about one knot now, but I'm using the time to rest. I don't want to alarm anybody, but I've had three or four bowel movements today, and I'm bleeding inside somewhere. I don't know whether it could be my stomach. It's feeling pretty good right now, but it was feeling lousy. Yesterday and the day before it was like an acid stomach. I've drunk the rest of Beau's milk, and I'm trying to stick to a soft diet. I'm hoping a little rest will heal it. Maybe it's fatigue-oriented. I don't feel bad—don't hurt. I just perspire a good bit. I don't know what to eat next, and I'm afraid to irritate it, but I ate a little more during the day today. I'm afraid to take medication for diarrhea for fear I'll hurt what's bleeding. When I mash the ends of my fingers, they don't stay white. I've been told that if they did stay white it would be one sign of a bleeding ulcer. So it may be minor, whatever it is. I'm hoping it will take care of itself.

I did a lot of little things around the boat today. I got the other jib sheet out in the cockpit so I can use it to reef the genny when I want to bring it down to 110 percent. I put in the reefing and I got a block out. Everything seems to be well-organized. The little Bimini top is holding up well. It's a godsend, and I have Tommy's to fall back on if anything happens to this one.

My noon shot yesterday put me off Savannah. You won't believe this, but I was within two miles of the course I plotted before I left home and within two or three miles of my dead reckoning position. My navigation seems to be right on, and I'm making a much better course this time than last time.

Fran's Log:
We drove over to the yard this afternoon so I could give them the damaged goods. I told the manager about the chronometer and that I would like for the person who touched it to know that we knew. He was sure that it had been the mechanic and indicated that the man had been fired. I told him that that was not what you had wanted—that you had suggested that he have the damages deducted from his paycheck. I added that I wasn't so charitable as you and that I thought anyone who didn't realize that someone's life could depend on the quality of his workmanship and his integrity had no business working in a boatyard. He agreed with me and we parted on amicable terms.

He was also very enthusiastic about wishing you luck on the voyage and said he certainly would like to have something from the boat for a souvenir when you get back, even if it was just a screw. I thought that would be an appropriate item to give him.

After that we went shopping, and I bought a book called *The Dollar-Wise Guide to England.*

At nine tonight I was out on the porch sending love messages into the northeast. I hope you and *Folly* and Jake are sailing fast. I miss you, but I'm still feeling good, and I hope you are. I feel close to you.

DAY 4: *TUESDAY, JUNE 14*

Log:

> Noon position 33°05′.6N, 75°22′W. Day's run 20.
> I rested in cabin. Slept possibly nine hours. Lost some
> distance, but hope the trade-off was good.

0730   Set course of 80-90°. Doing about 2 knots. Sea calm.
> *Folly* taking care of herself.

2200   Heard porpoises blowing around the boat.

Tape:

1850. The sleep last night felt good. I had a bowel movement
during the evening, and it was bloody, too, and like diarrhea.
This morning I decided to go ahead and take medication for
diarrhea. My stomach is settled—no upset stomach. Bowel
movement this morning was bloody, too.

At noon I went below to get the sextant, Nautical Almanac,
and sight reduction book. I was perspiring a lot in the cabin, and
it wasn't that hot. I bent over to get a pencil out of the drawer.
The next thing I knew I was down on the deck. I had passed out
for a couple of minutes.

If the weather had been bad, I don't know how I would have
gotten through the day. I'm afraid I'd have panicked. But I've
been working on this, and I can talk right now. I feel a little
woozy, but it's not as bad as it has been. My nails look better.
There were times when I looked at them and thought they
looked awfully white. After I squeeze the ends of them now,
they quickly go back to pink, so I may be on my way to overcoming this. I've taken two more diarrhea pills, and if I can
control that, maybe it will slow down the bleeding.

I want to tell you, the bleeding scared me. I've been calm
about it. When something happens to your innards, you really
are surprised. I've never had anything like this in my life. I don't
know how long a person could bleed like that and get away with
it, but I don't expect it could go on too many days.

I would be afraid to head for land right now for fear I would
be weak close to land, and that would be dangerous. Even if I
hurt myself out here, I'd rather hurt myself than somebody else.

I'd rather take my chances out here. This may take care of itself. I have to feel confident right now that I'm overcoming it, and I think I am.

I haven't listened to the radio except for the day I left and this is Day 4. I brought out Gert's tape of Mozart, and I might listen to the other side of it tonight. I played the harmonica for about thirty minutes this morning. Really bad.

DAY 5: *WEDNESDAY, JUNE 15*

Log:

Noon position 33°23′.7N, 73°23′W. Day's run 68.

1200 Feeling better. Caught almost two gallons of water from squall this morning and washed my shirt.

Tape:

2110.   I got a lot of little things done today. Did everything I wanted to do except shave and cook tonight. I ate a couple of peaches for breakfast. Got a can of potted meat and made a sandwich. For lunch I was hungry for sardines, and I got a lemon and put part of it on the sardines and made lemonade with the rest. It was good. I was feeling pretty good. My stomach started burning this afternoon. I was going to have Spaghetti-o's for dinner, but I got out some pudding instead to try to keep my stomach passive.

I think my stomach may be where the bleeding came from. I just pushed a little too hard this time. I was trying to think why. Before I left, for one reason or another, I had to be discourteous to everybody—family and friends. All of that really made my stomach burn, and I guess it all caught up. They all just got to me. The last week at home was so pressed with last-minute things and final exams—right down to the end when poor Little John climbed the mast to put on the new telltale and there was nothing he could do up there. I want to say all these things now just to get the anxiety out of me and forget it.

I wish we could explain in a book somehow that when some-body tries to do something like this, people should try not to rile him too much because he has so many things on his mind. I was sharp to you a couple of times, and I just didn't want to be sharp to anybody.

After spitting this out tonight, I'll be better. I'll be able to relax, and we'll be able to laugh about this tape later. I love you. I was going to shave today and couldn't find time.

The weather has been pretty out here, and out of Wilmington they say we are supposed to have two more nice days at least. Maybe I'll get around Hatteras without anything bad.

DAY 6: *THURSDAY, JUNE 16*

Log:

Noon position 33°54'.9N, 73°48'W. Day's run 61.

0525   Awoke feeling human again. Hurrah! I knew it had to happen. *Folly* tending herself well under 130% genny and first set of reef points in the main.

0817   We're getting off east of Hatteras.

Tape:

0817. If we're lucky, I'll get in before August 6 for our wedding anniversary. But if the weather decides different, I'll get in when it says I can get in.

DAY 7: *FRIDAY, JUNE 17*

Log:

Noon position 35°24'.7N, 72°32'W. Day's run 100.

0720   Blood not nearly as bad.

0920   Took reef out of main. Threw bad carrots out of box and discovered another peach.

1445   Weeping from sheer joy of feeling normal. England, here I come.

1600   Finished *Alice in Wonderland.* Started William H. Bligh, *The Mutiny on Board H.M.S. Bounty.*

1900   COOKED. A meal fit for a king—Spaghetti-o's. I ate the whole can. Listened to Norfolk, Virginia, on the radio today. Now listening to BBC.

Fran's Log:

Mother and I went to Waycross today and got our airplane tickets to London. We couldn't get a reservation for August 1, so I got it for August 2.

We did a little shopping, and I bought a yellow nylon windbreaker. It won't take up much room in my seabag.

In the bank in Waycross I saw the sister of a boy who was in my class in school. She said she had seen the newspaper articles and the TV coverage about your trip. She said, "It really gives you a lift when someone you know is involved in something like that."

I was out walking on the beach and looking your way and thinking about you at nine tonight. I feel anxious sometimes because I want you to know that I'm all right. I miss you so much, but want you to be doing what you're doing.

I have the chart you left for me with your route marked off in segments taped to the wall in my room. I marked off another two segments today, and there are an awful lot of segments between Hatteras and Plymouth.

Day 8: *SATURDAY, JUNE 18*

Log:

	Noon position 35°22′N, 70°24′W. Day's run 121½.
0130	Awoke with burning stomach. Took some Mylanta. You don't suppose my cooking didn't agree with me?
0200	Ship off port quarter.
0940	Big tanker passed off our bow about ¼ mile. I don't think he saw me. White superstructure and black hull.
1400	I shaved and spruced up. Humanizing.
1900	Pancakes were served for dinner. My compliments to the chef.

Tape:

2200. We're beginning to get a little breeze. We've been becalmed about an hour, but we've had good winds. I enjoy making over one hundred miles a day—three times this trip. We aren't too far from Bermuda. I could scoot over there in a couple of days, but I'm north of it now. In ten or twelve days I'll start on my second great circle route. Then I'll be off the Azores. It sounds strange to be saying that. The trip's going well. On our distance we're about six hundred miles down course. I'm doing better than eighty miles per day. I might get there a little ahead of schedule. I've moved into another time zone.

I think the bleeding has stopped. If I can just get my strength back and not feel drained, this ought to be a piece of cake. I'm cooking and keeping up with the dishes. I'll have to do some clothes washing. It's been a week.

I'm getting into more of a routine with my sextant shots. I take one about 0900 and then I get a noon shot and combine the two and I've got my position very close. My navigation is right on. I'm really enjoying using this sextant. It's a nice little instrument.

DAY 9: *SUNDAY, JUNE 19*

Log:

Noon position 35°12'N, 68°18'W. Day's run 84¼.

1005   Just figured my morning shot, and with a great deal of luck, I could make the trip in a little over five weeks. I won't count on it. Sixty days is what I expect. Fifty-one to go.

Peanut butter crepes for lunch. That's peanut butter on cold pancakes. And a cup of chicken noodle soup.

Making 5¾ knots with wind on our starboard quarter.

Jake is doing great.

1900   Chili with onions and red pepper flakes for dinner. Weather now gusty with lightning. Barometer steady.

Tape:

Midnight. I had a salty dog with dinner. I put salt around the rim of the glass and poured in grapefruit juice and rum—the first cocktail I've had on the trip, and I enjoyed it with my chili. Afterwards I slept until almost midnight.

Now I'm picking up WNEW out of New York.

I listened to a soccer game this afternoon. It was played at

Shea Stadium. I used to pass by there often on my way to Mamaroneck to teach.

Getting a good ride on a reach. A little squall going by now. I've been able to stay in the cabin more today because it's cooler. I don't have to wear the harness down here, and I feel freer. I read a little bit. My stomach hasn't been very acid today, and I enjoyed feeling good. I feel as if I have more energy, and that's a triumph.

I got the Brasso out. Maybe I'll clean the lamps tomorrow. I cleaned the chimneys today and washed the dishes.

I get a lot of satisfaction from my day's navigation work. Ours is the type sextant to use on a boat like this because the horizon doesn't jump around, and it's not too heavy. I'd recommend it to anybody for this size boat. I'm getting to the point where I can look and see what we've traveled, and I can predict very close to where we are. That's what navigation is all about—good judgment—and my judgment is getting better and better. This is a good place to learn.

At night I run with the 130 percent genny and one set of reefing points in the main. Yesterday the wind was so strong that I didn't take the reef out. I've taken it out once or twice, but I put it back in the evening.

I've really been enjoying this. You said, "Go out and enjoy it," and that's what I'm doing. I'm unwinding from shore life. I'm feeling well tonight. I'm getting normal again, and I have a good appetite.

I sponged off with some of the water from the rainwater jug, cleaned my nails, and babied myself a little bit.

Fran's Log:

Good news today. Beau called this afternoon and said he has made a good contact in the Coast Guard office in New York. He gave me the officer's name and phone number. They had your float plan and now have attached a note to it to call Beau or me if anybody reports seeing you.

The other good news was that according to the Weather Bureau, the weather offshore has been good, and you've had plenty of wind.

Beau is terribly frustrated that you don't have a radio. He says

he can't let you leave on another trip without one. He wanted to
know if it made me anxious that you didn't have one. It doesn't.
I never expected you to take one and haven't given it much
thought. I might be worrying if you had a radio and we were not
hearing from you.

Beau is writing a follow-up article for tomorrow's *Atlanta
Constitution* and wanted me to help him pinpoint a possible
position for you as of tomorrow. We decided on 36°N 68°W. It
will be entertaining to see how far wrong we are.

DAY 10: *MONDAY, JUNE 20*

Log:

Noon position 35°23′N, 66°21′W. Day's run 126¾.
Bermuda having bad thunderstorms. Winds gusting to 50
mph. Hope those were the ones that passed me last night.

2230   BBC program on explorers. Sir Edmund Hillary said, "I
endure, so I conquer." God, does that mean something to
me now.

Tape:

1920. I opened a Coca-Cola to have rum and Coke with dinner. There was a little Coke left, so I'm having a little more rum
and Coke. This drink is pretty strong. I didn't know the Coke
wouldn't fill this glass again. I'll be relaxed tonight. This rum
and Coke is saluting Bermuda—a little bit of Georgia, too, with
the Coca-Cola.

The storms got me up two or three times last night. Poor old
Jake just couldn't override the big gusts so I went out to help.
Then I remembered I had those beautiful blocks so I put one on
each side with the ropes running from the tiller to the companionway. I just reach up and pull on a rope and help Jake from
here rather than having to go out in the cockpit to bring her
back on course when she's blown off. Much better arrangement.
I'm getting fancier.

I read some more of Captain Bligh today and rested after
being up so much last night. The temperature is pleasant, and

it's nice in the cabin. I sat outside for about thirty minutes this afternoon. Otherwise I've been inside.

I'm listening to the BBC. They're playing "Swan Lake" and it's nice. But I've been listening to Bermuda all day, and that's a good station. A lot of good music—some good classical music this afternoon. Really fine. Now I'm catching up on my English news so I'll be prepared when I get there and fit right in. I get a time hack from BBC as well as British information. At midnight they'll give international news again in sections—world news, UK news, British Isles news. It doesn't seem that important out here, but I'm keeping track of everything. Then they give all the cricket results. I'd like to see a cricket game while I'm in England, especially if there's somebody there to tell me what it's all about. I remember seeing a cricket game once in Hong Kong. I'm looking forward to having several weeks in England just to enjoy relaxing and traveling around and seeing the country— getting to know the people. I have no urge at the moment to get home quickly. Having the boat in Europe will be nice. We'll have a reason to go there.

It's very satisfying to be able to take a project like this and so far to be able to bring it off well. I'm happy about everything we did on the boat for seaworthiness. I haven't wished for anything. The Bimini top could blow out, but it does everything it is supposed to. It is designed just right. If I asked a man to make one, that would be the design.

The deck leaks that we worked on are holding up beautifully. There's no water discomfort. One or two waves let a little bit of water in through the hatch last night, but nothing too bad. I've noticed a little water in the bottom of the liquor locker. I didn't drill a drain hole in that one.

Fran's Log:

This afternoon I finally settled down to some writing. I've started an article. I feel good about that.

I marked off another place on the chart. That's always a cheering thing to do. I've been getting along fine. I just feel slightly unreal. It's a long time to be without you. I hope everything is holding up all right on the boat—that the stove is working and you're using it and that the caps to those fuel jugs are OK.

DAY 11: *TUESDAY, JUNE 21*

Log:

Noon position 36°23'.1N, 63°54'W. Day's run 110¼.

Tape:

2330. We're going to entitle this tape "Storms." Learned a major lesson today. They've been reporting thunderstorms with fifty-knot winds around Bermuda. I figured we were catching them around here already, and I was handling them all right with the 130 percent genny and reefs in the main. I had to help Jake four or five times during the day to get back on course. Well, this evening I started cooking a little earlier—around 1700. I got everything out and thought we were going to have us a meal, starting with Courvoisier and soda and cracklins before the shrimp gumbo.

I had the Courvoisier in a glass on the table, and I had gotten the French bread out. I had the shrimp gumbo on the stove heating with rice—good gumbo, just like back home. Tabasco was on the table. I was going to have a feast. Then I got hit by a thunderstorm that just laid her over. There was no controlling her. The cockpit was taking water, and the winch handle compartment on the low side was filling up. I think that's where the water backs up and comes down into the lower locker, especially in the liquor locker.

Anyway, I had the forethought to reach down and shut the stove off when I thought it was really going to be rough. I got up to the companionway and was trying to help Jake, and I just wasn't doing any good. Then I slipped and fell against the stove. I felt the heat from the pot of gumbo, and why it didn't scald me, I don't know. But I broke both gimbals, and we had gumbo all over the place on top of the counter. So here I was with water coming over the cockpit. It was a mess with everything heeled over, but everything on the boat was staying pretty well in place.

One of those corks that stop up the drain in the back was floating around the cockpit, and I thought I was going to lose it. It
was funny my pulling on that rope to try to bring the boat up to
save the dumb little cork, but it was something to focus my
attention on.

When I finally pulled her up, more water was pouring out of
the locker and going down into the bilge, so the first thing I did
after I backed the sails and we were resting more comfortably
was to take care of the bilge. Then I took all the water out of the
liquor locker. I left the sails aback so the water kept draining out
of the holes in the lower port lockers. Three yellow writing pads
were on the deck, all wet. I cleaned up the gumbo mess. And I
knew I had to get up there and reef the genny. And the wind
was strong.

When I went out in the cockpit, I noticed a block was busted—
that other turning block like the one that broke on the starboard
side last summer. I reached in here and got another spare block.
So right now, of the six spare blocks, I have one for my jiffy
reefing on my genny on the bow; I have the two white ones back
here in the cockpit for my self-steering; and I have one now
replacing the turning block. So I have two spares left. I sure was
smart getting six of those things instead of skimping and getting
two, because now I'd be wondering what I'd use.

I'll be able to repair the gimbals with some tap screws when it
calms down. I've anchored the stove down. I'm sure it will work
fine. I'll just have to fix the gimbals. I scratched my arm some
and bruised my side when I fell, but not bad. I'll live.

I hesitated about getting up there in all that wind, but when it
happened, I got my winch handle and went up there and went
through the routine. You just have to be awfully careful. You
have to do a balancing act to get the new sheet in the new clew. I
don't care for it a great deal, but I managed it. I'll get better at it.
Your mouth gets plenty dry. But I had thought about it and
planned it so it wasn't bad. And I even had to change the broken
block back there on the port side.

The purchase I had on the boom worked real well for putting
the sails aback. I have one that keeps it so I can't jibe the boom.
Everything was good. I just left too much sail up too long. Ear-

lier in the day I should have gone up there and reefed the genny. I just kept putting it off, telling myself I would do it before it got dark. I think that was the reason I was eating earlier.

I had to stand on top of the life raft to be able to reef the genny. Thank God that life raft is where it is or I'd never have reached that clew. I could lower the sail first, but I'd rather have something in that clew to have control. That's another thing I've learned cheap. I was lucky. And thank God I'm rested and my health is good now.

Needless to say, after I finished the reefing and the cleaning up, I ate the little bit of cold gumbo left in the pot. I wouldn't be robbed of it. And I had another light Courvoisier and soda. I had only had about half of the first one. The rest of it dumped out on the table.

Folly handles a lot better now that she's not so pressed with sails. Jake takes care of it for the most part. My bunk is dry—hurrah—and I have some dry clothes to put on.

DAY 12: *WEDNESDAY, JUNE 22*

Log:

Noon position 36°19′.1N, 61°15′W. Day's run 118.
Barometer 30.40. Amen.
Bermuda news says 40-foot yacht *Imp* being rescued by Coast Guard out of New York. Lost rudder approximately 156 miles NW from Bermuda. Five aboard all OK. I know what bad weather did it. I've been through it. Beautiful now. Drying out everything.

1630   Fixed gimbals on stove. Things pretty well dried out. Time to fill the lamps and trim the wicks.

1830   Had pinto beans with rice, asparagus, tomato juice and rum. Meal fit for a king. No incident!
Did a lot of work today. Hope to polish lamps tomorrow. Boat looks respectable again. One turning block is only casualty of bad weather. *Folly* is really a great little ship. I could never have a finer craft. I only hope I always own as good a boat. I am fortunate.

2200   Wind shift to west. I'll run along on this course (approx. 130°) overnight then change over to the other reach tomorrow. I hesitate setting the whisker pole and running down wind. Especially at night.

Boat moving comfortably

DAY 13: *THURSDAY, JUNE 23*

Log:

Noon position 35°56′.2N, 59°57′.5W. Day's run 65½.

Changed from starboard to port tack after over 1,000 miles. About 460 miles from second great circle route.

1300   Set wrist watch ahead one hour. Three hours' difference from Greenwich.

1730   Tied loose reefing point on genny. Replaced broken reefing point in main. One slide broke loose. Will fix when becalmed. I have spares aboard.

Lost all vegetables except potatoes, onion, apples, and peaches. May be some cabbage good.

2230   I've lost track of a jar of peanut butter. It was in the bar. Might be there yet, but I couldn't see it. If it went into the garbage can, I threw it overboard. Maybe during my cleanup after the stormy weather I threw it out. Feels like *The Caine Mutiny* and the missing strawberries. I opened a new jar of peanut butter. I can't make the galley slave walk the plank if he did throw it out.

DAY 14: *FRIDAY, JUNE 24*

Log:

Noon position 36°37′.5N, 58°16′W. Day's run 67¼.

Oiled and reset log at noon and made and ate a whole pot of cush-cush for lunch. I'm as content as a kitten after feeding. Stove alcohol consumption very light.

High pressure center close by. Within 60 miles of ⅓ mark. Averaging 92.7 nautical miles per day on log. Outside possibility I'll make it by July 23.

P.S. Found the peanut butter.
Still haven't polished the lamps.

DAY 15: *SATURDAY, JUNE 25*

Log:

Noon position 36°39′.4N, 57°25′W. Day's run 105½.

1030   On starboard tack. Really rough going, but heading in the right direction—more north. Need a real dodger over the hatch.

1130   Back on a reach. Too hard going on tack. Wind changing to SE. *Good!*

1320   I'm on a reach and will lose ground, but I'm cruising, not racing.

1500   Wind trying to swing more to the south. Rain front coming from the west. Wind should shift more. We'll see in the next few hours. Hope it swings around to the south or southwest.

1825   Just finished dinner—beanee weenies, rice, and milk. That topped off an uneventful day. Think I'm putting a little weight back on. Maybe I'll get a wind shift tomorrow. Where are the westerlies? It's just not worth beating to weather. I could go on a tack now, but if the wind freshens after dark, I'll be miserable. If the wind won't cooperate, I hope it will stay quiet. Read a little more of Bligh today.

1900   Shaved and the wind shifted some more. Maybe I should shave each day.

Fran's Log:

Two weeks today, and I think I've reached a new plateau. Either I'm less anxious or I'm getting used to it. Everything just has to be all right where you are. I keep thinking of meeting you in Plymouth.

DAY 16: *SUNDAY, JUNE 26*

Log:

Noon position 37°42'.7N, 58°14'W. Day's run 125.

Tape:

0120 (6/27). Two big happenings.

I was fixing dinner and looked outside and there was a tanker. It was getting dark. He started signaling with a light. I can't read Morse code that fast so I got out the code book and my hand lantern and I signaled "ZDl" two or three times. I think the flash he returned was that he understood. I guess he noticed I couldn't find anything in the code book that said, "I'm OK; don't bother," or anything like that, and I couldn't read his lights. Then she went on her way, heading west. She could have been going to the Chesapeake or New York.

Now we're going to find out if the Coast Guard gets all upset about my signaling "ZDl." I should be reported to New York. Beau ought to be hearing from me if he calls tomorrow and asks about it. I just hope to God the Coast Guard doesn't think I'm in trouble and come out here and make a fuss over me. I could have signaled to notify Lloyd's, but we're still on this side of the Atlantic. I took a couple of pictures of the ship. They didn't get close enough for me to see the name, and I didn't grab the binoculars to look. It was pretty windy out, and I was just being sure that the boat stayed on course.

At 2100 the wind came up. It was a front coming through. I had to get outside at 2115 and help Jake for several hours. He just couldn't hold it up there. I put on my foul weather jacket and went out, and I was there until twenty minutes ago. It blew. And it rained. I know we got some winds up to fifty knots at least. I managed to keep the boat pretty dry. I put a life jacket over the opening of the hatch. We got a little water over on the galley. It got far enough over to touch the tape recorder, but it just sprinkled it. I don't think it's going to hurt it.

The best news yet is that we've shifted from a compass reading of about 350° to almost 40°. Doggone it, if that wind isn't going to shift around to the west now. That's very pleasant, and it might even moderate after this front goes through. I can do

110° and be happy because we have 20° variation here. There were a lot of wind storms in the front. No thunder and lightning, though, thank God.

I hope signaling that ship gets word to the Coast Guard and that it doesn't catch somebody there who thinks, "Oh boy, a sailboat's in trouble," and they wonder about me out here. If they read the book right, it's the same kind of signal—just above "Report me to Lloyd's"—so they know where I am. I hope I don't hear anything from it. That way I'll know Beau got the word, and you'll hear. You'll see that I'm pretty far north of my track, but if they check the weather, they'll find out we've been having southeasterly winds, and they're pretty strong out here. They should moderate some now, and with a wind from the western quadrant, I can make some easting.

If I could head due east, I'd be happy. I'm still well to the south of the Grand Banks, but I don't want to get too close. I think the weather gets sloppier up there. We are supposed to have westerlies up in this section.

Fran's Log:

I went sailing today—finally. After lunch I decided to find out what all the other sailors were doing on Sunday afternoon. I went to Dell's first. All the boats were there except the *Christopher.* I couldn't get mad at them for not asking me to go because I don't know them very well. Then I went downtown. All the boats there were in and closed up. Nobody around but sightseers. I looked at two transient sailboats and was heading back to the car when a voice behind me said, "Let's go sailing." It was Jake. He and Jacob were running toward the *Anna Maru.* I followed and jumped aboard. There was a good breeze. We sailed out to the sound and back. It was fun. Maybe if I hang around the dock and look lonely, I'll get asked again.

The first fellow in the singlehanded race to Bermuda came in. Ninety-eight hours in a forty-footer. I almost think I could have—well, not ninety-eight, but I made pretty good time to Bermuda coming up the coast, and I lost a lot of time when I was sick. Glad that didn't happen when I was in the storm.

I marked off another two segments on the chart today. That would put you northeast of Bermuda and due south of Newfoundland. Jake asked if I had figured how long it would take you at the rate I'm marking off the chart. I said no, that I wasn't thinking farther than three days ahead. He said you'll be there forty-five days from June 11. I hope he's right.

Beau called tonight. He checked with the Coast Guard again. No reports. He also checked the weather. The weatherman said the chances were that you had been in at least one fairly severe thunderstorm with winds thirty-five to forty knots. He also said there is a weak low-pressure system moving off New York at about 20 mph and that it could intersect your route about mid-week. He said it shouldn't be anything major but could increase your winds by five to ten knots.

This is something I read in *Motor Boating & Sailing* (April 1977) this afternoon. It is in an article by Hal Roth:

> Nothing can compare with the accomplishment of the solo sailors who—when the going is tough—have no choice but to carry on. As one seaman once put it: "When they are tired there is no one to take their watch; when they are anxious there is no one to relieve them of their anxiety; when they think they are sick there is no one to laugh them out of it; when they are fearful there is no one to lend them courage; when they are undetermined there is no one to harden their resolve, and when they are cold there is no one to hand them a warm drink.

I love you, Love. And I don't just think about it at nine o'clock. Beau says he thinks you're a little less than one-third of the way across. That makes it seem like an almost manageable amount of time.

DAY 17: *MONDAY, JUNE 27*

Log:

       Noon position 39°53'.5N, 57°53'W. Day's run 138.

0845   Woke up. Sails aback and it's beginning to rain. Totally overcast. The seas seem to have moderated a little. Got a morning sextant shot.

1200   Heading 110°. If this could hold for three or four days,

I'd be in good shape. The westerlies were rough coming, but maybe they are here to stay. No noon shot. Too overcast. Sun has come out since. It's beautiful.

1600   Slept an hour and a half this afternoon. On a comfortable riding reach. Could sell sailboats today.

2000   Light rain shower and wind gusting.

Tape:

2130. No Coast Guard today, so if Beau called during the day I expect that you've heard something about my whereabouts.

I've started reading Agatha Christie. *The Murder of Roger Ackroyd.* It's a good book. If it holds my interest as much as it has so far, I'm afraid I'll have to read more Agatha Christie. I could get hooked on fiction.

I had time to meditate today about all the things we've done like choosing the stove and picking a sextant and the reasons why. And the headsail being 7.25-ounce material and being able to reef it so well. And the tie-downs on the stove. This stove works just fine in all sorts of weather if you can just keep from falling on it. And the grab rails and the lamps. The cans and preservation of the food. And the variety is nice, too. I have plenty of different things to eat aboard.

As of today we have 1,574 miles on the log in sixteen complete days. That's almost 100 miles a day. I've had three days of 130 or better; three days of 120; four days between 100 and 120. Ten days out of sixteen that were 100 miles or better.

This hull really moves. And tracking downwind with the keel the way it is and the skeg rudder, that's terrific. She's a seakindly little boat. The waves had to be twelve or fourteen feet or better. I would say ten to fourteen feet. I don't want to overestimate them. When we got down in the troughs, they were way up above us, but that stern just rose to the occasion. I had just one wave slightly break over the stern. The rest of the time I was able to keep her pretty level. She tried to go on a reach only twice, heeling over and getting lee rail down. It was just a matter of keeping my eyes on the compass.

Last night the wind got so strong it blew out the stern light. I don't have a bow light on. That ship that passed yesterday was in a slow shipping lane from New York, and I'm between the lanes now. I think my cabin and stern light give enough light. I can throw on the electric lights if a ship approaches me.

I've set up some codes in the cover of the code book in case Morse code comes in again. It's just that those fellows on the ships flash that stuff so fast I can't read it.

DAY 18: *TUESDAY, JUNE 28*

Log:

Noon position 38°33'.7N, 55°47'W. Day's run 141¼.

0100   Winds up a little. We are not heeling excessively. Handling it OK. Sailing about 120° true. A little more than necessary. I've let up on the main a little and put the helm more to weather; that might bring us up a few degrees. The moon is spectacular tonight.

0720   Slept about 4½ hours in a row. I was a little tired after the storms. Really big swells out from the west. Wind pretty strong.

1000   Best day's run yet—141¼ miles. I never thought I'd make a run like this. Mostly in the right direction. Really high seas. Jake doing the job well. I helped three or four times this morning.

1800   Waves are 14 feet. We are really moving along.

Tape:

2100.   No Coast Guard today so I hope they are aware of what the situation is. No ships around, thank God. They should be south of me.

With our little plan of your marking the chart you'll be just about up with me. Another four or five days, and I think I'll be at the halfway mark, and I'll have a bottle of champagne. Then it will be downhill. We're comfortably south of the Grand Banks, and I haven't noticed fog. I feel very good about my navigation.

According to the wind roses on this part of the ocean, this weather is abnormal. They indicate force 3, and this is more than force 3. Those waves have been running hard for a long way because the wind has been blowing a long stretch over the water to get waves up this high. This isn't just a local thing. I'm glad we have all first-rate equipment. I wouldn't want to be out here with anything shoddy. It's enough of a ride with good stuff without having to worry about your gear.

I hope your days are going well and that you're getting everything done that you want to. Your nerves ought to be unwinding by now with me gone seventeen days. I hope you've heard from the Coast Guard. I would like to think you have some general idea of where I am. I've been thinking of all the things we can do in England.

Fran's Log:

We went to Brunswick today and reserved a car. It will be waiting for us at the London airport. We've leased it until September 6.

I can't contemplate everything's not being all right so I think of your enjoying everything on the boat and feeling good because you are making good time.

DAY 19: *WEDNESDAY, JUNE 29*

Log:

Noon position 37°59′N, 53°26′W. Day's run 146—a new record.

0030   Went out to reset Jake and discovered one of the two lines holding the log was cut through and the other one about gone. I tied a new one. That was close. I worked Jake until 0400. He was having a terrible time staying on course.

1000   Tanker off to port heading west.

1200   I didn't sleep much last night, but look at the day's run. I really worked for it.

1930   First calm day in several. Sure have been busy, and I'm very tired. I'll take a little nap. A nice day like today restores my faith in the weather. Barometer is up and the waves are down.

2200   Beautiful night and gorgeous full moon. I wonder if Fran is enjoying it.

Tape:

2230. At 1100 I took the main down and replaced four slides that had blown out. I resewed the two hand-sewn ones on the top. I had two to screw in, and then I checked all the screws on the slides of the reefed main, and sure enough, some of them were loose. Then I ran the main back up and it looks nice. I was lucky. Every slide came down. None of them stayed up on the track. Didn't take me but about thirty or forty minutes to do the work on the cabintop. That came from being prepared. I had everything set up. I even took the screwdriver and taped a piece of rope to the handle and tied the other end off on my safety harness so if I dropped it, I wouldn't lose it. I had a butterscotch pudding as a reward for my deck work. It was the last pudding on this side, and I'm not going to the other side until I get to the halfway mark. Then I can start enjoying the treats I have on that side.

At 1700 I filled the stove for the second time since Florida and cleaned the galley. The stove was still only about half empty, so the consumption is very low for cooking.

I put a longer rope on the end of the boom so the boom can't jibe. If I had had that on last night, I could have slept a little better.

There are forty tall ships in a Silver Jubilee race from England to France in forty-eight hours. The Queen went down to Falmouth and saw a parade of naval ships. My little crossing here is nothing compared to all the big doings for the Silver Jubilee.

Fran's Log:

I wonder if you're seeing the big moon or if you are in the low-pressure system that the weather bureau said would intersect your course about midweek.

Gert just called from Montauk. They have been sailing along the north shore of Long Island, and they go on to Block Island tomorrow and then to Mystic. It sounds like a lot of good sailing. Since hearing about that, I'm feeling envious again. Oh well. Back to Sea Sand. I cleaned the garage this morning.

DAY 20: *THURSDAY, JUNE 30*

Log:

Noon position 38°19'.4N, 51°28'W. Day's run 99.

0900   Just woke up. Really slept last night.

1050   The weather today is what you dream of as island sailing.
Gentle breeze, low, rolling sea with little wavelets and
perfect temperature. There was never a more perfect
morning. I'm very rested. What I had to go through to get
here was truly worth it. I only wish I could transport Fran
here for this moment.

1100   Standing at the hatch thoroughly pleased with myself
after breakfast, and I burned a small hole in the Bimini
top with my cigar. First cigar accident. Mended the top
with duct tape.

1425   Just finished *The Murder of Roger Ackroyd*. Great mystery. I guessed the murderer two days ago. Good to see
my brain has not grown soft.
Lunch was sardines with lemon and fruit punch. Dinner:
tequila and tomato juice with hog cracklins to stimulate
appetite, crawfish bisque—the real thing with four stuffed
shells—and fresh cooked rice, topped off with a glass of
hot tea. No man ever ate as well going across the Atlantic. Bless everyone who had a hand in my diet. One ban-
quet after another. I've started reading Josephine Tey's
The Daughter of Time. It's good.

2150   I put on a pair of long-sleeved pajamas tonight. They are
comfortable and fresh. Really living high.

Tape:

2300. The wind is shifting from west to southwest, putting us
on a more northerly heading, but it's going to bring me around
the Grand Banks all right. The barometer is reading 30.50, and
that's high. And I'm in my highest compass variation—22°. I'm
going a bit more north than I want to, but the self-steerer is
comfortable. And I'm cruising, not racing.

I've traveled 1,960 miles as of today. I'm ahead of my eighty-
mile-per-day schedule, so I'm a little ahead of where you have
me on your chart.

Fran's Log:

I miss you. I hope you're farther along than my chart indicates.

I got some books from the library and have started an Agatha Christie.

We got a letter from Malvina today. She says she has written Lloyd's but hasn't heard from them so she has written again.

DAY 21: *FRIDAY, JULY 1*

Log:

Noon position 38°57′.1N, 49°28′W. Day's run 72½.

0600 "Go east old man." So I am. We have come north enough. Now to get over to our second great circle. A little more overcast today and wind up one notch. Wind shifted to south. Low must be passing to north of us. Wind coming over starboard side again. First lump of oil found on starboard sail block track on deck next to cockpit. Nasty.

1300 I'm on my second great circle. A little over 2,000 miles to Scilly Isles. Look out, England, here I come. We will see if winds cooperate. They are doing beautifully now. Barometer is high but very overcast at noon. Almost never got my noon shot. Didn't need a filter on the sextant.

1730 Looking over the chart. I could arrive England in 23 more days or better. That would be terrific run. Reread the red notebook today. I'm in good shape. Cleared up about 1400. Very clear now.

Tape:

2310. Happy July 1, baby. It's Canada Day today.

Just had a ship pass off to port. I turned on my running lights because I think my stern light has blown out. She was fairly close. I could see all her running lights. I'm sure they saw me. She seemed to slow down. This morning at 0700 a big, black-hulled freighter came by on my starboard side. I'm in the low-powered shipping lanes, I think, between New York and Europe or the Azores. I ran up "ZD1." If someone was watching with binoculars, he saw it. I ought to get out of these lanes in the next day or so. The high-powered lanes are farther north. Those ships make me nervous when they come by. They might pick up my radar reflector on their scope. Just so they don't run me down. They can see I'm not in trouble because I'm making time to the east, and I'm going on. The horizon is all clear now. I left "ZD1" flying. If a ship comes by when I'm sleeping, they can see that and report me. Maybe by now you are getting some word and seeing that I'm a little ahead of schedule. I would fly the flags "Report me to Lloyd's" if I knew Malvina had taken care of that with Lloyd's again. When I get farther north, I'll start flying "ZD2."

I'm proud of the boat. She's still holding up nicely. I had blown one reefing point out in the main. I guess I blew it out again. I'll have to substitute that lighter line I have on the spool for one of the reefing points. I am happy that headsail is that heavy material. The other one is, too.

Tonight the wind was strong enough to blow over the canvas cover on the vegetable box on deck. It really howled for a while, and we were running downwind. Moitessier said in his book that he preferred to carry a little sail and run before it as long as he could. That's what I did, and it worked out right fair. I wouldn't want that to go on for a day or two, though.

DAY 22: *SATURDAY, JULY 2*

Log:

>   Noon position 39°18′.4N, 47°W. Day's run 112¼.
>   Remaining fuel 19 gallons. Water 56.

0700   I woke up to find us bounding along on 140°. I did a controlled jibe and got us on 80°. We are now on a port running reach. The barometer dipped early this morning but is up again.

>   I got 6 hours' sleep last night.

1800   I shaved this afternoon and look pretty again. Weather nice yet. Barometer still up.

Tape:

2255. Over the ground I've gone 2,124¾ miles. Tomorrow or the day after I'll hit the halfway point.

My stomach has been ornery and cantankerous lately. This afternoon I went through the whole medical kit to find the Riopan. I finally found them. I have a package of sixty, and that's good. I took one, and it works better than the Mylanta II. The Riopan and the four Mylantas left ought to hold me to the end of the trip. I'm not using much but my stomach flares up every so often.

This afternoon I heard a French program on CBC. They were featuring Cajun music from Louisiana. They had everybody from Kershaw to Kenneth Richard and Big Boy Broussard. I could pick up enough of the French, and they were discussing how the music in Louisiana was a lot like the music in Canada except it wasn't as old in tradition. The lyrics are about that part of the country. One of the songs was updated—kind of like rock. Then they played some regular old-fashioned Cajun music with steel guitar, and they talked about how that was affected by Texas. The music made me lonesome. I wept when I listened to it, but it was good and I really enjoyed it. In Canada they don't use steel guitar, and we do, but the sound is still there. It's the same music.

They interviewed a woman who had sailed across the Atlantic in the transatlantic race, and now she's getting ready to crew in the Whitbread Round-the-World Race. They also interviewed a Canadian singlehander who was in the transatlantic race. He singlehanded over to Bermuda. The biggest boat in that race was lost. They moved a radio beacon in Bermuda, and several boats hit a reef because they were following the beacon at night. The doctor who owned the boat that was lost was hanging around Bermuda to see who would be legally responsible because the contestants hadn't been informed of the relocation of the beacon.

I heard a dramatization over BBC called "The Wolf." Their shows are like old-fashioned shows when we were kids. They read the different parts from a book or story. I listened to the Armed Forces Radio this morning, but they play little strip excerpts of things they tape, and I don't care for it. BBC is much better organized, and I'm really used to the Canadian station during the day. CBC is in French, English, Inuktitut, and Cree. I've been listening to them so long I'm at home with them now. I've picked up BBC in Japanese, I think, and I even heard Radio Moscow for a while tonight.

I relax a lot out here now since I have everything pretty well set, and I'm into a routine. I get the meals up, do the navigation and piloting, see that the boat keeps heading in the right direction, and do everything to stay alive.

No ships today, thank God. I don't care to be around those ships. Last night that made me sleep lightly. Maybe I'll relax more and sleep heavier tonight.

I'm sure by now you have gone to Waycross and had the car inspected, and you've gotten your flight tickets. The marina knows we're not coming back now. We're into July, and I'm still out at sea. You might have gone sailing today. If not, maybe tomorrow.

Fran's Log:

My days are busy, but I certainly do miss you. Right now I don't look too favorably on a round-the-world trip. I'm not sure I can get along without you for ten months.

I've mentioned to several people that I found two conchs on the beach, and when I told them I left them in the water because I didn't want to kill them, they just looked baffled.

The mark I made on the chart today puts you into your second great circle route. I think you've probably been doing better than my 240 miles every three days.

DAY 23: *SUNDAY, JULY 3*

Log:

Noon position 40°14′.4N, 44°52′W. Day's run 108¼.

0045   Just finished *The Daughter of Time*. Good book.

0715   Really slept soundly from 0100 to 0700. Today looks like the halfway mark to Scilly Isles. It's a beautiful day. This is the fourth straight day of good weather.

1400   Just set my local time ahead one hour. Two hours' difference between *Folly* and Greenwich. Hooray! It's downhill now.

1800   Shackle pin came out of shackle on jib sheet. I had spare sheet in cockpit and rigged it quickly. I have an old shackle that I can rob the pin from. Shackle all fixed. Took about two minutes. Thank God the wind was light. That genny could have done itself some harm while it was loose. I have several galvanized shackles I can use, if I need them. Third gear failure on trip. Not bad. The turning block cracked on the port side, and sail slides popped out.

1845   Stomach fair today. Sky clear. Ocean calm and beautiful. Barometer still nice and high.

2030   Sunset and BBC playing "Dance of the Seven Veils" from Strauss' *Salome*. Like a dream world. Wish Fran were here for this moment.

Tape:

Midnight.   This evening was my halfway-mark dinner. I had champagne in a champagne glass, chicken chow mein with noodles, and a glass of hot tea. I took two or three pictures of the feast.

At 1200 a tanker looked as if she came off course to look at me. She got within two or three miles of me. With powerful binoculars they could have seen me. They might have picked me up on their radar screen and wanted to see what I was. She was heading east. I was glad she didn't come any closer. Right now, being becalmed, I wouldn't want a ship close to me at all.

Started reading *Night Flight* and that's good.

I changed the batteries in the radio today. A set of batteries lasts a week playing the radio every day. And I do play the radio a lot. It gives me company. It's a luxury I can afford to let myself have. I still haven't polished the lamps. The one over the galley is a real mess—kind of greenish.

I've just finished another box of cigars.

Fran's Log:

I'm not interested in a round-the-world venture unless it includes me and stops at every port.

Beau didn't call tonight so he must not have heard anything, and he knows I would have called him if I had. At the rate I'm marking the chart, you'll get there July 23.

I love you. I hope *Folly* is taking good care of you.

DAY 24: *MONDAY, JULY 4*

Log:

> Noon position 40°58′.7N, 44°30′W. Day's run 33.

1145   Finished *Night Flight*. Good book.

1410   Started Sir Alec Rose's *My Lively Lady*. Overcast now but barometer high.

Tape:

2345.   Happy Fourth of July! I hope you got to see the fireworks tonight and that you thought of me. I hope you enjoyed them for both of us.

I tried to start the engine today, and the battery was a little too low. I put in some of the battery fluid—VX-6. I had to empty one of the cells a little to put it in. Maybe the battery will recharge. The engine looks all right. I'll keep trying from time to time.

This morning I sealed the portlight over my bunk with silicone sealer on the outside. It was just an annoying little drip when there was a lot of rain.

It's nice to have enough stuff aboard to try, like the battery fluid and the silicone sealer, and to be able to go right to it. With the chart you made for me; there's no problem, and I sort of remembered where they were.

This is the fifth day that I haven't had any foul weather. I keep thinking we're getting up in the north Atlantic so anything could happen any day. But that's not necessarily so. It could stay pretty for several more days. The barometer has dropped down to about 30.40 in the cabin, but it does that at night. It's overcast and pitch black out now. Can't see the moon.

Who knows? Another nineteen or twenty days, and I could get to England. On my course right now I'm doing about 130°. That's about 110°. Doesn't make any difference, though, because I'm a little north of my line. I can run three or four hours until daylight like this. It's a little more south than I have to be going, but it will be OK.

I'm gaining on the Azores. They're due east of me. That's my closest port now. We're moving on and chipping away at it. That thirty-three miles yesterday didn't take much of a chip out of it, but that's going to happen once in a while. I won't get upset.

I might cook pancakes for breakfast tomorrow. The leftover pancakes keep well in one of the pieces of Tupperware that I emptied when I finished the grits and oatmeal. I'm usually awfully sleepy in the morning, though. It takes me about an hour to get my head unwound and get going. I have a cigar during that hour and drink some grapefruit juice or pineapple juice or whatever I pull out of the locker. Then I'm ready to face breakfast.

After breakfast I do my morning shot. Then I read and relax, and all this time I have CBC on. Then I reduce the morning shot and plot it on the sheet and note what the log reads. At noon I crawl out and reset the log. Then I usually read for an hour or so. I shoot at 0900, and by 1000 I've finished working out everything and studying the chart, and I get mesmerized and daydream about the chart a little.

At 1100 or 1200 I read and really pay attention to the CBC. I go out around 1300 for my noon shot. I'm out there ten or fifteen minutes while the sun goes across the meridian. Then I come in and work out the noon sight. That's not done on the long sheet. You just correct it and get altitude correction and subtract it from 90 and get the declination and add to that. Then you know what latitude you're on. I take the plotting sheet that I plotted the morning position on and move it forward the number of miles in the direction we've traveled since I shot that morning. I apply the noon shot to it, and that's my running fix. It's right accurate, I think. It's not bad. There have been only two days that I couldn't get a noon shot. I've been lucky.

After all that I cook lunch and eat and relax until about 1500.

This morning instead of reading I went out and sealed that portlight and did other things. No two days are exactly alike. I haven't played my musical instruments except that one day when I was sick. I guess I ought to find some time for that, but I've been reading, and I'm enjoying that.

Some fool in New York has hijacked a bus—killed a couple of people.

Fran's Log:

Happy Fourth of July, love. I wonder if you're celebrating.

I went sailing today. It was a pretty day with a light breeze. Enough to sail but nobody had to work very much. We sailed up to Dungeness and back.

After supper we went to see the fireworks. I really missed you then. They were good, and you would have liked them.

I'll be glad when this weekend is over. The beach is mobbed.

Beau called tonight. They had spent the weekend at Lake Lanier. He said they were in one bad storm and broke out the life jackets and safety harnesses. He said they were glad to get in and have electricity and hot water. They thought of you because you have to keep slogging on after your rough weather.

DAY 25: *TUESDAY, JULY 5*

Log:

Noon position 41°11'.2N, 43°1'.5W. Day's run 82.

0130   Went out and did controlled jibe from 140° to 90°. Changed chafing gear and relit the stern light. This should bring us close to great circle route. That wind sure made a shift. The barometer went back up again.

0755   Woke up at 0430, then slept on to 0745. I must have slept about 6 hours altogether. Boy, did I sleep heavily.

0910   A freighter came around me. I should be reported now.

1630   I hope by now you have heard about the sighting of me. It's slow going now, but the weather is beautiful.

Tape:

1925. Big day today. I saw a freighter way off on the far horizon, and she was moving west—really tearing along. Then I noticed she was turning and coming over to me. She must have been about three miles away, but they spotted me. They made that turn so fast the ship heeled over. They were sharp to see me.

I grabbed the camera and power hailer. They came around to the side of me about a hundred yards off and circled me twice. I talked over the megaphone and said, "Twenty-four days out of Florida, going to Plymouth, England." He called back in a foreign language, and it was just no good. We couldn't understand each other.

I pointed up to the "ZD1" flags. He read them and went off around my bow. I thought that would be it—the last I would see of them. They made a big circle and sat off for a little while. Then they came back and looked as if they were trying to get an identification of me because they had binoculars and were looking at me. I enjoyed seeing other human beings around and having them look at me and know I was alive.

I kept pointing to the dodger and the stern and giving them thumbs-up and A-OK and saluted them and everything else, and I just continued sailing on to the east. They went very slowly by my stern and sat off on the horizon. I know the stern is hard to read and of course English would look as foreign to them as the language on their boat looked to me. "ZIMC]" was painted on the side of the freighter. It looked like Russian. There was no national flag flying. They could have been going to Cuba. I just continued to sail away because I didn't want to cause any trouble, and I didn't want them to think I was in trouble. Hope I didn't take too much of their time.

That's the second ship that I know has definitely seen me. If they report me, you'll see I've come a long way since that last ship. Our little formula is working out pretty well. I didn't make but eighty-two miles today, but I'm happy enough with that. I'm still a little ahead of my eighty-mile estimate.

The sea is rather calm, and the wind is not more than force 1. We're heading about 70°. I really want to be doing 80°, but that's close enough. We're heading closer to the wind than we usually can because the seas are calm. I was flat becalmed for an hour or so this afternoon. I had to take in the log. It went straight down. That was a little aggravating. I think it's the second time that has happened.

To me my position is far up enough to be getting the westerlies, but I'm sailing with a southeast wind now. I think these are just very weak lows going over me. That's all right. That keeps all the other mess like high winds and big waves away from me.

Only twice I've caught really bad easterly winds and was pushed way off of my great circle—once around Hatteras and the other northeast of Bermuda. All the other times I've been able to stay fairly close to the great circle. I expect I'll have covered 4,300 to 4,500 miles by the time I get into Plymouth. My estimates of the distance will have been just about right. That will be by log, and when we are going this slow, the log doesn't always record exactly right. It works well over two knots, I think. I don't worry about it. My sextant always brings me back into line, and for the most part it corroborates my run and my dead reckoning. My dead reckoning has been good. We're about to get over one more fold in the chart. After we get over that, there's just one more fold before we get into the European sector.

Funny thing about my watch. It had been losing time—running slow. Now it's running fast a little bit. The old chronometer was five seconds off. Now it has gained a second. It could be a temperature change.

I hope your days are going well. Tonight at 2100 I'll sit here and meditate about you and hope you have a chance to do the same for me.

I'm over halfway through Sir Alec Rose, and I'm enjoying it. Every time he's in the Channel, he has lousy weather—fog and gales—as much in July as any other time. I'm not worrying about it too much now. I'm not even worrying about the engine. It makes good ballast, and I know it's not frozen up. If it doesn't start, I'm sure someone will give me a tow to get in or I'll find an anchorage.

There have been some pretty men-of-war floating by. I should have taken some pictures, but I haven't. If I get the camera and myself and a man-of-war in the right position, I'll take a picture of it.

I hope I get to call you before August 1. Who knows, I might get spotted close to England, and you might get word about how close I am and decide to come over early. We'll have a ball being together in England. I can't believe it. England.

Fran's Log:

I look forward to getting on an airplane and heading in your direction. I sent messages at nine. I love you.

DAY 26: *WEDNESDAY, JULY 6*

Log:

Noon position 42°26'.6N, 41°13'W. Day's run 81.

0200   Just had three pancakes, strawberry jam, and milk. I woke up at 0100 perspiring. It may be warmer than I think. I sleep under the sleeping bag.

0300   Heard a "bang" on the starboard side. Thought something in the rigging had broken. I just checked. All OK. Beautiful night. Must have been a board in the water. I've seen a couple on the trip. I'll sit up a little while. I'm not very sleepy now.

1030   Wind up to force 3.

1415   I got the sextant a little wet doing noon shot. I washed it with fresh water.

1830   Just finished *My Lively Lady.*

Wind is strong and seas running high, but I'm making 5⅔ knots in right direction, 60° to 70°, on a beam reach.

DAY 27: *THURSDAY, JULY 7*

Log:

Noon position 44°8'.5N, 38°55'W. Day's run 144½.

0230   Started Thoreau and listened to Gert's classical tapes. There is something wrong with the Beethoven. The Mozart works well.

0830   Put on storm jib. Motion rough but tolerable. We are being tossed around a lot. Seas very rough. Sky clear now. North of Milne Bank and it's rough as all get-out.

1230   Too much spray breaking to go out and take noon shot.

1615   A good-size wave broke over the cabin. A little water came in. This is about the fourth one this trip. Seas are

still pretty rough, but the wind is down a little. Most
probably will get stronger tonight.

Tape:

Midnight.   Today has been a stormy day. I brought the 110
percent genny down and put on the storm jib. Took me thirty
minutes. I had rigged it once at Dell's, but I had never put it on
underway. We're on a starboard reach now with storm jib and
reefed main, and Jake's able to handle that just fine. The wind
moderated around 1800 or 1900, but I knew it was going to
come up again, and sure enough, it did.

When I was putting the storm jib up, I must have turned my
watch stem a couple of times because by the time I came back
in, it was July the ninth instead of the seventh. I hoisted the jib
once and the snap shackle that was holding the sheet on came
off because it was flapping around so violently. I had to bring it
back down and hook it up again and tighten up on the sheet
before I put it up so it wouldn't rattle around. That sail looks
small up there, but it's enough to balance the boat. I think we're
still making hull speed or close to it—five or six knots. We're
traveling at about 80° now. We were traveling at 70° before. I'd
rather be heading about 100°, but there's no need to try to work
any more to windward. This is enough, and she's more comfortable here.

I really got drenched up on the bow putting on the storm jib. I
had my foul weather top on, but it wasn't zipped up as it should
have been. I had about six seas break over me, and they wet me
good. I didn't realize it was as cool as it was. So I got everything
done up on deck and all tidied up. I have the 110 percent genny
still hanked to the stay because there is a rope tail on the storm
jib, and I put it on above the genny. I have the 110 percent
lashed on top of the 150 percent genny with half-inch line.

I came back down and dried out. I broke out a new pair of
socks and a shirt and took out my robe in case I want that. It's
getting cooler.

When I first put on the storm jib, I felt that the motion of the
boat was a little rougher, but that could have been just psychological. It's just a matter of riding it out now. There's no smaller
sail for me to put up. If I have to, I can heave to. With the 110

percent we would heel excessively to leeward hove to. We're making time in the right direction, and when you're doing that, there's no need to heave to as long as the boat can take it without excessive strain. I think everything is taking it pretty well.

The Bimini blew out completely today. I think the sun had finally gotten to the material. Everything has blown out but the ropes. We got our money's worth out of it. When the sun was really hot, it did its job. The silicone sealer I put outside the portlight seems to have done its job, too. I still have a dry bunk to sleep in. If I can stay warm and dry and keep fed and just be as comfortable as I can, that's the main thing.

Fran's Log:

I got a letter from Malvina today. She said Lloyd's had written her that they would be glad to report to her if anyone reported your position to them. She'll send me a cable if she hears anything.

I wrote the Mayflower Marina today to tell them you should be on schedule.

I'm beginning to feel that I can start looking forward to seeing you within a manageable length of time.

DAY 28: *FRIDAY, JULY 8*

Log:

Noon position 45°14'.1N, 36°W. Day's run 157¼.

0650   Totally overcast. Seas are still high and winds very fresh but not as gusty. Two waves have broken into the cockpit since I got up. Maybe it was just the shift in my body weight. It is noticeably cooler this morning.

1440   The wind is shifting to the south, but the waves keep us from holding 90° or better. The waves should adjust directly to the wind shift. I'm making splendid time under reefed main and storm jib. This is the longest day's run yet. Unbelievable. Ride not bad except when wave breaks over boat every 5 minutes or so.

2300   The wind just won't come from anywhere but the SE.

Tape:

2330. I thought the wind would shift today. It didn't. It's back up to snuff again, still blowing from the southeast. We're making 80°. I'm going farther north than I want to. My chart just goes so far north. I don't want to run off of it. I just wish it would shift or drop down so we could go on a tack. There's no tacking in this. I may have to tomorrow, but it will be rough sloshing if we do. I'll see where we are after my noon shot.

I was going to celebrate being two-thirds of the way in the trip. I had some tamales for lunch, but when it was time for dinner, I just wasn't hungry. I didn't have the champagne. In the middle of the afternoon I had a Coke and a little rum. Somebody drank some of my rum before I left and depleted the rum supply. I'm about out of rum. But that was my celebration this afternoon. My stomach kept acting up so I didn't have anything else.

I haven't taken down the Bimini top yet. It's all in shreds. If I go out in the cockpit, I just get drenched, so I don't go out there any more than I have to. When I can get outside comfortably, I'll change my flags to "ZD2". But if anybody saw me with this torn Bimini top, they would think I was a derelict.

One reefing point in the main is cutting through again. I'll have to change that. It has surprised me how those things chew through.

It's a little cooler. I stayed in my foul weather gear all day today. I guess I'll have to get out my winter clothes soon. I have both cabin lamps burning, and that makes it a little warmer. The one in the back will stay on when we're on a reach like this. I've wrapped the sleeping bag around me, and it feels good.

The Queen's gift and the proclamation are riding well and doing just fine. We'll have a good time in England when we get there. I hope you and your mother are planning things to see in England. It's just going to be lovely to be with you.

Every once in a while the boat will give a little lurch and you'll hear the dishes shift around. She has different sounds on different points of sail—different things rattle. She's doing just fine. Really kicking up her heels and scatting along. I hear the spice jars rattling. When I hear that, I think we want to travel east more. They are my easterly sounds, but when I looked at the compass on the table, we were going in the same direction.

The news gets discouraging. Another plane hijacked.

Fran's Log:

Four weeks tomorrow. I hope you're OK and happy. All I can do is imagine that you're well and happy and having a wonderful time sailing.

Joe Caldwell called and said the *Jacksonville Journal* is going to do a short article with a map indicating where we suppose you might be.

I love you. I miss talking to you, among other things.

Now that I've heard from Malvina, I've been thinking that the chances of your being sighted and reported to Lloyd's are greater from now on, and maybe we will hear something.

I've been lying in the hammock reading mysteries, and I've been walking on the beach every day.

DAY 29: *SATURDAY, JULY 9*

Log:

     Noon position 46°15′.9N, 33°25′W. Day's run 152¼.

1550 We're doing OK to windward. Doing about 6 knots at times. Listening to BBC.

1830 We had a light shower and the wind is coming up again.

Tape:

2000. I got up at 0600 and found the sails aback. We were lying quiet in the water, and the wind was really blowing. I found out then that with reefed main and the storm jib, the boat really heaves to nicely. I put on my foul weather gear and went up in the cockpit and put us on a starboard tack on about 110°. We've been doing that all day. This ride is a little wet and the going may be a little slower, but I'll have to put up with it for a couple of days. Well, we are headed the right way.

The wind has died down to about force 1. Right now I could

have a lot more sail up, but I'm not going to get up there and worry about it tonight. I'll see what happens tomorrow. As long as we're clipping off good daily runs, there's no need to mess with anything.

While I was in the cockpit at 0600—sort of twilight and overcast, wind blowing and big waves—I looked around me, and I was right in the middle of a school of pilot whales. I got the camera and shot some pictures from the companionway. Waves were breaking over the cockpit so I didn't want to get out there with the camera. They were right off the stern, pretty close. They dove through the waves and played around the boat for about an hour putting on quite a show. They weren't as big as the ones I saw off Hatteras. There were adults and babies. I enjoyed them. They were a beautiful sight. They were fascinated by the log, but they never bit at it. They would just dive at it. They would jump right out of the waves.

The log read 124¼ miles at 0600, and if I took another reef in the main, I would have storm sails up. I thought on a tack we wouldn't make as good time, but at noon we had covered 152¼ miles. That's 6⅓ knots. My God, that's really moving. I've never moved in a boat like that before—yesterday and today. I was shocked to see the distance we made under storm jib and reefed main. I couldn't believe the log when I read it. I took my sun shots and they verified it.

During the afternoon I made a cup of hot tea and put some Courvoisier in it. That's a fine drink. Tonight for dinner I had salisbury steak and gravy with leftover Chinese noodles and another one of my special drinks. I took a vitamin pill this evening. I put some Tabasco on the steak—trying to seal up my ulcer.

At about 1515 I got out my winter clothes and put on my green sweater and my watch cap. That makes me a lot warmer. The two cabin lamps make it warmer in the cabin at night. It's brisk out in the cockpit compared to the cabin. It's about 65° inside and 55° outside. I have my boots on and my foul weather bottoms.

We have a bit over 1,000 miles to go yet. With a little luck we should get there in a couple more weeks. As of today, my trip average is 91¼ miles per day. Over the ground it was 103 miles.

I'm into my new set of reduction tables—45° and up. I'll wait a while to get the sailing directions out and start poring over them and my charts. I haven't tried the engine recently.

I think the boat will be in good shape when we pull into England. I manage to keep up with everything, and the gear seems to be holding up well. I haven't gone into my food supply on the other side of the boat yet. I should have plenty of supplies left when I get to England. We'll have some to use when we're there.

You should have gotten at least two reports on me. I haven't seen a ship in quite a few days. I should be between the lanes now, and I'm hoping not to see any. I'll begin picking them up in about another seven or eight hundred miles.

I wish you were here during the good times. I'd rather you wouldn't be out in the rough weather we've had. You'd take it all right, though. It wouldn't bother you. When you're by yourself the weather isn't as much fun. With two or more aboard, with somebody to keep watch, it wouldn't be as much of a strain. Alone, it puts you under a bit of tension because when you're sleeping you don't know what's going on. So far—knock on wood—if a shackle has come loose, it has been when I was awake. But things don't always go wrong only when you're awake.

This is the North Atlantic. I just don't know where all the westerlies are, but I don't need a westerly now. I'm doing just fine with my southeasterly. The barometer has dropped to about 30.55. In Florida 30.40 is normal. This may be normal here.

I haven't caught any weather forecasts for the English coast. BBC gives lots of time hacks but no weather. Since it's cooler, my watch and the chronometer have started running faster. It's nothing to worry about as long as I can keep track of it.

I've been reading Thoreau. I agree with him in part on some of his points. It's interesting reading and easy reading. That surprised me. I didn't know it was going to be easy.

Fran's Log:

Sometimes I'm a little afraid. Tonight my fears seem to be coalescing. I'm afraid of what the trip might have done to you and for you. I'm afraid that the total aloneness might have been more than you bargained for. I'm afraid you'll get to Plymouth and never want to set foot on the boat again. I'm also afraid that I will have missed too much—that you will have had this big adventure and experience and will have gone off on some other plane and left me crocheting and walking the beach and reading. And then I'm afraid you will have had such a super time and will have loved it so much that you can hardly wait to set off around the world alone.

These worries don't do you or me any good right now, so when I finish this, I'll crochet a belt to wear with my new pants.

There's an article in this afternoon's *Jacksonville Journal* about you.

I think you ought to be directly north of the Azores now. That's a little ahead of what I have marked on the chart, but I'm figuring (and hoping) that you're making better time than that.

Sometimes I feel as if I've spent a lot of time complaining. But this experience hasn't been all negative for me. I read a book once by a woman who had spent seven years in a Soviet prison, and after it was all over and she was out, she wrote that she had to say that the experience had added to her life rather than taking away from it.

I've done quite a few things I've wanted to do—like doing an honest piece of writing—and I hope *Sail* buys it. And doing some frivolous reading. But also I think I'm more the real me than I've ever been before. If I figure out a way to define that further, I will.

At the same time, I seem to be developing a twitch in my left eyelid. (That's a good name for my book.) I've looked in the mirror while it was twitching, and it's invisible to the naked eye, so I guess it's an imaginary, psychosomatic twitch.

I love you.

DAY 30: *SUNDAY, JULY 10*

Log:

Noon position 46°15′.9N, 30°13′W. Day's run 132¼.

0130   Winds up and sounds like rain. We are really moving along in the right direction. The waves seem not to be breaking *too* bad. This must be a squall.

1045   Another day or so and maybe I can get off this tack. It is
       rough at times. Got a good night's sleep.
1240   Changed to 90°. Maybe the ride will be better.
1605   I'm comfortable and the ride is a little easier. I'm really
       not complaining. We're making decent time.

Tape:
2215.   Everything is slipping and sliding. I have a cup of tea
in my hand—smoking a cigar. It's raining out. Wind still southeast. We're bouncing along making about 85°. We've come into
15° variation so that's about 70° true. Ninety would be better,
but it's a rough ride.

We have had a lot of squalls since 0130. Waves are breaking
over and keeping the galley a little damp at times. I put my
sou'wester over the stove to keep it dry. While I was doing that,
all of a sudden I noticed that the blue sailbag that's lashed on
deck on the port side was dragging in the water. I put on my foul
weather gear and went out to stow that. The front part had come
loose and doubled back and was dragging. I managed to get it
inboard, doubled it over, and tied it to a handrail. That was a
wet job with waves busting over.

We're over another time change, but I haven't changed my
watch yet. That will put me three hours different from Florida
and one hour different from Greenwich. I figure it's approximately 960 miles to the Scilly Isles. The way we're going on, we
could get there pretty quick, but the weather is always subject to
change.

According to BBC, Wales has been having a heat wave—80°—
and trouble with a brewery strike. Pubs are running out of beer
and people are getting a little irritated. Hope the strike doesn't
make it so bad I can't get a pint of bitters when I get in. I'm
looking forward to seeing a real English pub.

Yesterday I heard the Mormon Tabernacle Choir singing the
"Hallelujah Chorus." That was beautiful. There are a couple of
good classical programs. They've been kind of hot for Elgar
lately, so I've been hearing a lot of Elgar.

For dinner tonight I had macaroni and cheese, and I put lots
of bacon bits in it. To start with I had some peanuts and a bottle
of champagne and enjoyed watching it bubble up in the glass. I

celebrated being 75 percent of the way. One more bottle of champagne to celebrate with when I get close. We'll have the big bottle when you get there.

The end of the American ensign has shredded out again. I'll be able to save that one and pin it up on the wall to remind me of the winds up here. We'll have a lot of memories of this trip.

With a boat this size, I think I'm doing decently. That track behind me is getting longer and longer. It dawned on me today that this trip is about as far north as I've ever been.

Fran's Log:

Jake called this afternoon and asked me to go sailing with him and Anne. We had a nice sail out to the black can near the fort and back. It was beautiful.

DAY 31: *MONDAY, JULY 11*

Log:

Noon position 47°05'N, 27°52'W. Day's run 116.

0725   It's noticeably cooler today and thick overcast. Maybe it will clear for a shot at the sun. Progress very slow at the moment.

1315   No noon shot but good latitude shot at 0900. Approximately 870 to Scilly Isles. England, here I come, though rather slowly.

1600   We are moving about 2½ knots. This will lower my daily average, but we knew that could happen.

Tape:

2120. I moved my watch an hour ahead today—just one hour different from Greenwich Time.

The wind has dropped down to force 1 and has switched around to the northwest, believe it or not. I got up at 0545 and changed to a port reach. When I was out, I heard a propeller plane overhead way up high. Must be going to Europe. It should have gotten there in an hour and a half. I'll take a little longer. I heard three of them today—one at 0545, another prop plane at 1315, and one at 1925. They could be flying to the Azores or

Bermuda. It was nice to hear human life outside. Getting back to civilization.

At 0725 I got out the bird book to identify the birds I had been seeing. There was a bird flying around making noise, and it was a new type I hadn't seen. It was a tern. During the rough weather the Wilson's petrels were around. They are storm petrels. I'll verify that! There's a sooty shearwater flying around behind the boat now. They glide a lot—hardly ever flap their wings.

It's cool outside. Inside it's about 65°, thanks to the little lamps, and outside it's about 10° lower. I'm burning both of them for heat. When I turn on the stove, it's to do some cooking. Both lamps seem to be burning very nicely now. I've gotten them straightened out—especially the one back here near the stove. It has a lot of green on it from being exposed to salt water, but that won't hurt anything. It's colorful. I haven't taken the Brasso to them.

Tomorrow I'll have to change the flag signal and take down the Bimini top. The Bimini top is a good scarecrow to keep the birds out of the cockpit. It's a good wind indicator—an old buddy of mine—but it will have to come down.

If any of those ships turned me in, you know about where I am. I'm a little ahead of where you surmise. By now you should be thinking there's a chance I'll get there before the first of August, but of course the smart thing to do is not to think about it. There are too many unpredictables.

I haven't tried the engine again. If it isn't working when I get to the Channel, I might try to send word to the Mayflower Marina to look out for me and come out and tow me in. I hope the weather will be good when I get around the English coast.

I've logged 3,131¼ miles. That's almost 4,500 miles altogether that I've singlehanded, and that was in forty-two days.

DAY 32: *TUESDAY, JULY 12*

Log:

   Noon position 47°20′.5N, 26°54′W. Day's run 44.
0938   Prop plane high.

1040   Approximately 820 miles to Scilly Isles. Our day's run
        will be low today. Ocean very calm and wind light.
1650   Got good sextant shots today.

Tape:

2130. I got up this morning at about 0800. We were pretty
nearly becalmed. I had a glass of tea, put my foul weather gear
on to keep warm, and went topside to change the "ZD1" to
"ZD2." I'll be reported to London now if anyone should see me.

One of the reefing points in the main had gone out, so I tied
another one in. I secured the big blue sailbag at the bow again,
took down the storm jib and set the 110 percent genny and set
the boat on a 90° to 100° course. The 110 percent genny is set
now with the main. I ran four or five days with the storm jib.

After the sail work I put pillows out to air, put some wet
clothes out to dry, and put dirty clothes away. Then I had breakfast: grits with bacon bits, and boiled egg, and a glass of hot tea.

I took my morning shot and worked it out and then tried to
feed some old biscuits to the birds. They wouldn't eat them—
wouldn't bother with them at all.

I can relax a little now. This afternoon I took out the short
pajamas and wore just the pants to sun myself in the companionway.

I tried to start the engine, but the battery was down too low. It
won't turn the starter. That acid didn't work. Then I tried crank-
ing it, but I can't crank it fast enough. That's all right. When I
get to England, we'll recharge the battery or get a new one. I
guess I could have turned the engine faster, but I didn't want to
strain myself. It's heavy enough. I turned it over a few times, so
it's not frozen, but there was no starting it, so I shut off the gas
and took out the vents in the back. The locker under the cockpit
seat is pretty damp. I'm sure moisture has gotten to the engine.
We'll dry it out when we get into port. It's all bedded down, and
I won't worry about it until I get in. It doesn't disappoint me at
all because I didn't plan to use it. I'll have gotten to England on
a gallon of gas.

We haven't made any time today, but being becalmed has
given me a chance to get ready for England. The boat has dried

out. It's comfortable. And I've had a lot of exercise—in perpetual motion all day. Everything is pretty well arranged. I'll save the fine cleaning for England.

I took some pictures of the ocean and the clouds—the way they looked when we were becalmed. And tonight just before sunset we were going under a front and I could see from one side of it to the other. I took pictures of that. The cloud bank was like a road over my head. It's cool again tonight, but it got up into the seventies today.

I moved the food from port to starboard, and this afternoon I had so much to choose from I couldn't make up my mind what to have for dinner. I was pleased to see when I looked under the port bunks that the drain holes I drilled had worked. There was no water standing in those lockers. Some of the cans are a little rusty, but none of them have gone bad. The forward locker on the port side is empty now. I took everything from there that I didn't move to the starboard locker and put it in the aft port locker, and that trims the boat a little better.

Tonight I had Courvoisier and soda and some cracklins; then for dinner I decided on crawfish bisque, rice, and the last French loaf. There was just one little bad spot on the bread so I took the bad spot off, and nine-tenths of it was good. I laced the bisque with Louisiana hot sauce—delicious. With the meal I had the other half of the soda and some Courvoisier. I don't believe anybody ate any better than I did tonight. Wish you were here to enjoy it.

Under the bunk that I'm sitting on now I've put all the grits and dried foods. I put the granola bars in the icebox. The eggs that I boiled are kind of soft in the middle, but they're good. I'm down to one pack of hot chocolate so I'll save it for a special occasion. Next time we provision for a trip, we can bring more of that, especially if it's going to be cool. I drank almost two-thirds of a pack of the cold tea mix today. That's how warm it was.

I've been listening to BBC all day. A Russian ship tried to go into Plymouth—it had gone into Plymouth before—but they didn't want it to go in there because NATO was having some sort of maneuvers off the southwest coast of England, and they thought the ship had a little too much radio equipment on it. I might run into the NATO maneuvers if they're out there long enough. Anyway, the Russian ship is going to Falmouth or Portsmouth. Carter has given the OK to continue research on the neutron bomb. That's big news in England. And the big cricket matches are over and England beat Australia.

You know by now that I'm making my way past the Azores— way north of them. I hope everything is going well for you.

DAY 33: *WEDNESDAY, JULY 13*

Log:

Noon position 47°48'N, 25°27'W. Day's run 68.

0420 Awoke at 0400 to find us doing 40°. Set tiller to put us on starboard tack, and it brought us close to our 100°. Watching sunlight creep over horizon. It's gorgeous. Ride very pleasant. Seas aren't too high. Going back to bed.

0845 Got up at 0800. Wind force 2. If this holds, we will make a little time.

I may read some today. Listening to BBC now, and I miss Fran so. We could relax together today if she were here. Oh boy, would that be fun. I'd better read a little now.

1400 Well, about 750 miles to the Scilly Isles. We are moving pretty well at the moment. If this wind holds, I could make 120 miles in twenty-four hours. Hopefully in the right direction. I'm not doing badly course-wise now.

I've started a manuscript to Fran—sort of an anniversary letter. She made such sacrifices for this trip. I will never be able to repay her. But she is the flower of my life. Maybe I'll talk to her in ten days or so.

Played the harmonica twenty minutes this morning and about ten minutes this afternoon. Very bad. I believe I drove the birds off.

1500 Just had a chocolate pudding party.

1915 Put kerosene in all the lights, and they are all lit.

Tape:

2200. I got out *Reed's Nautical Almanac* for the English

coast, and it's good. It has radio beacons, lights, suggested courses to steer between points, distances between points, tides, all sorts of good information. Right now I figure I'm about eight hundred miles away from Plymouth. I could get there in ten days—the twenty-third. I'll be getting into the shipping lanes in the next three or four hundred miles—maybe sooner, maybe later.

I guess one of the first things I'll eat, if I eat out when I get in, is steak. I wonder if an English pub has steak. Or some good bread. I heard a discussion with some Frenchmen about how the French have good bread because in a town they may have three bake shops. Because the industrial revolution hit England so early, they had bread made by machines, so there was no competition for the best bread. Who knows? I might be able to get a French loaf when I get there. I don't really miss all those things, but I'll treat myself to them anyway.

There's a lot of bird life up here in this part of the ocean this far out—more than off Florida, I think. It's surprising. It makes the ocean not so lonely.

I have had the steering lines running into the cabin for about three weeks, and I can handle most anything from inside. I look out at the ocean, and sometimes when we're rolling around, I can see the ocean through the windows. It's more comfortable. I stay drier in here and don't suffer from exposure too much. I've been using hand cream and my hands are in good shape. I have short pajamas on and my green robe and my sea boots and watch cap. Boy, do I look salty. I feel like Chichester in his smoking jacket.

These tapes are a good idea, allowing me to talk thirty minutes a day. Believe it or not, I don't talk to myself much during the day. I think a lot, but that's not like exercising my voice. I ought to be in rested condition when I get to the Channel. I'm not tired. I think I'm on English time now—their Summer Time. You'll be more tired from jet lag when you get there. My stomach has been in good shape for the last two or three days. I think my weight is about normal.

Each day when I get closer to England, my spirits soar a little more. In the evening when I speak to you, I'm pretty relaxed. As the goal gets closer, I get a feeling of more and more satisfaction.

Fran's Log:

Today is the first day since you left that I haven't had some definite project to begin or to finish. I've spent most of the day reading. That involves my mind and makes the time go faster. I've made efforts at writing, but my mind wanders.

I just came in from the porch. I was out there sending messages at nine as usual. It's midnight, I guess, where you are. I love you. That was the main message. Then I began worrying about your being so alone for so long and wanting you to be OK and enjoying the voyage, but afraid it might be more ordeal than pleasure. Then after about five minutes I got up and came inside. I can't let myself think about that.

If you still want to singlehand around the world, I'm going to have to find a way to make a life for myself separate from you between now and then. I'll have to find something I really enjoy doing that I can get paid for and that I'll have to go to work and do every day. Then I'll have to prepare myself to do it, if it takes any particular preparation. Right now I don't know what I would do. I guess Lady Chichester ran the map business and Lady Rose ran the grocery store.

I've gotten along fine here this summer, but only because I knew it wouldn't last more than two months. For any longer period of time I would have to be at home and on my own.

I think of your calling to say you're there and you're OK and of hearing your voice and touching you, and I feel better. The memories that come to me aren't so much of big things we've done, but just of quiet moments together—like holding hands walking on the beach and reading and eating popcorn in bed and drifting in the Sound becalmed.

The man from WGST radio in Atlanta called this morning to ask if I had heard anything and where I supposed you might be. I said possibly north of the Azores. He said the BBC had called them about a week ago to ask about you. They gave the BBC my address and phone number, but they haven't called me. I wonder if you've heard a report about yourself on the BBC. The British Consulate in Atlanta may have sent some information to them.

This morning I gathered up a few pieces of mail to bring to you.

Please be happy wherever you are.

DAY 34: *THURSDAY, JULY 14*

Log:

Noon position 47°40′.5N, 23°23′.5W. Day's run 129¼.

0230   Awoke. Wind shifted to west. Boat heading SW. Raining out.

0400   Changed to port running reach. Lay back down.

0500   Wind rising. Light rain.

0845   Clear with sunshine. The waves are a little rough. I'd hate to go on a port tack now. If only things would quiet down a little. I wish the wind would shift more westerly. Well, we can't have everything.

1515   At 1400 I changed to a port tack but not a hard tack. If it doesn't change, we can hold what we have. I have about 700 miles to the Scilly Isles and 800 to Plymouth. BBC mentioned gale force winds in the Channel. I hope it's nice when I get there. I'm satisfied with the day's run. Not all in the right direction, but it brought me back to the great circle route.

Tape:

0130 (7/15).   Happy Bastille Day, baby. Vive la France!

Riding on a port tack is different. It makes the world topsy-turvy. I had been on a starboard everything for so long.

I'm pleased about the course heading right now. The seas were heavy today, but not as bad as they could have gotten, and after we got used to being on this tack, it was all right.

Yesterday's run was sort of an arc, but it brought me right back to my great circle. There have been a couple of shoal areas that I skirted to the west. I didn't care to go right over them. I never knew how bad the weather was going to be. When I get to the Channel, there will be some places within ninety miles of the Scilly Isles where it comes up and there are some more shallow spots. Nothing I have to worry about, but when the wind whips up, it gets rough around them, sort of like the Gulf of Mexico. The waves should build up pretty big around there. I'd just as soon avoid them if I can. I think there were three of them on the trip that my track would have gone right over. Now it's all clear to the Scilly Isles. The variation will drop, so I expect I will keep about the same compass heading, but I'll be heading a little more east.

The north wind was so cool that I took the little white top that I made to put over the hatch and I tied it onto the handrails, leaving a slit in the top at the companionway. That helped some. The sun warmed things up considerably today. And now the wind isn't blowing directly into the cabin.

The BBC carries a lot about the States. The big blackout in New York, people looting. They talk it up. But you have to watch the British commentators. They interviewed one man about how far the civil rights movement had come since King. He said outwardly it was a little better, but inwardly it was about the same. And that's not true. The country really has changed a lot, in housing and education, jobs and pay, and in a lot of ways. They played it down. That surprised me. That was one thing they have discussed that I knew a little about in our part of the country, and they were underselling it. The news isn't always so good. There were mixed stories about a helicopter that has been shot down in Korea. If it's not that, it's assassinations or hijackings or kidnappings.

If you have marked off two of those 120-mile blocks every three days, I'm ahead of you on the chart now. You might be surprised when I call.

DAY 35: *FRIDAY, JULY 15*

Log:

Noon position 48°11'.8N, 20°55'W. Day's run 103¾.

0240   Wind shifting to the northwest. Will go on broad reach in the morning. Listening to Madrid, Spain. English broadcast for Americans.

1100   I got up at 0745. We are now running before a west wind. A little past 0800 I got a morning sun shot. We are making our way toward England—about 680 miles to Plymouth. After working the shot, I had breakfast: grits with bacon bits, grapefruit juice, boiled egg, and a glass of hot tea. Then I shaved, trimmed my mustache, and cleaned my fingernails. I also just cleaned my cigar holder. I'm now having a second cup of tea while writing. It's cloudy out but the barometer is very high, and the seas are nice. All is well this morning.

Sure miss Fran, but I'm getting closer. I'm getting even with the northern edge of the Bay of Biscay (latitude) and halfway to England from the Azores (longitude). I'll be getting out my charts soon to study the Channel and ports, including Plymouth. Next Friday I could be off the coast of England. I still can't believe it's me out here, closing England. Hope the weather holds to Plymouth.

I have the companionway two-thirds closed with a white canvas I rigged. I'm in my robe, pajamas, and sea boots. I can't let a ship see me like this. I don't want anyone to think I'm weird! I have a sweater and my long pants ready to put on. Already starting to think about civilization again. Well, I look pretty—shaved and hair combed. I look rested, too. My face might be a little fuller, and I might have gained a pound or two since I left. I feel very fit. My legs may be a little weak when I get in, but it shouldn't be too bad. I'll find out when I step on terra firma.

Last night before I went back to bed, I tried AM radio, and I picked up Spain, Germany, France, and England clear as a bell. Also some middle eastern countries. I'm getting close. No FM radio. AM held much better than shortwave. However, shortwave has really improved in the past few weeks. I enjoy BBC, although after a few hours, it's repetitious.

I have now reached the conclusion that Columbus' voyages might have been somewhat enjoyable. They had each other for company. For me, in order of hardness to bear, the main difficulties have been: (1) being away from wife and people, (2) finding out how *Folly* reacts to different situations, (3) my health—bleeding and acid stomach—I think I've now managed an ulcer or two—and last but by no means least, (4) doing all the things I have to do for myself—cooking, etc.

(1) I haven't been able to overcome loneliness for my wife. I'll arrive quite sane, but parting from Fran has not been "sweet sorrow" but sour each day. I hope she can rejoice in my accomplishment this summer. I've learned and verified so much I thought I knew. I'm feeling a great deal of satisfaction when I look at the chart and see how far I've come and how well I handled each situation that came along. I have no reservations about taking care of her at sea. The trip was worth it just for that. I can take Fran around the world safely and she can be thoroughly confident in my ability. And I now know that the way she and I handle ourselves on *Folly* is very professional.

(2) *Folly* has handled everything beyond my wildest expectations. She is truly a fine and fast sea boat. Quality equipment certainly makes a difference. She is worth many times what we have invested in her. She would stand on her head to take care of you. I really believe she loves deep water. Lots of personality and all good. I could kiss Robert Finch of Sparkman & Stephens. He could never design a better boat this size. Too bad they don't build them any more. And I can't rave enough about Jake. He works so very well and hard and never a moment's trouble or complaint. We were smart choosing this design. I couldn't be more indebted to a group of people than to those who built him. He is sturdy, reliable and strong. The strength is very comforting out here. Waves actually broke against him, and he took it like a champ. Bravo *Folly* and Jake! I'd recommend the combination to anyone without reservations.

1415   I went out at 1220 for noon shot. I looked up and there was a black freighter, port side heading east. First in ten days. I think he slowed down and looked at me. Didn't come close. With good binoculars they should have been able to see my flags. Maybe they saw me shooting my noon shot and figured if I was doing that, I was all right. After I got my shot, I jumped down in the cabin and put on my pants in case they came over to me. I'll dress each day being close to shipping lanes. I really got excited. I've changed the battery in my hand lantern. I want a good bright beam for signaling. Saw a couple of terns outside after lunch of tomato soup, rice and tea. I'm about to have a can of fruit cocktail.

(3) My health really gave me a scare at the beginning of the trip. I would have asked about medical assistance if I could have talked to a ship during those days. I had never passed out from a health problem before. I know I wouldn't have closed the coast. It would have been too dangerous for me and others who might be called to assist me. I couldn't count on staying conscious to make decisions. As it turned out, I was able to cope, and I shall never forget it as long as I live. The stomach pains were bearable, but passing out really came as a shock. I had no warning that I could recognize. When we get back to the States in September, Dr. Syn can see what damage, if any, needs repair. I will take his advice and do or have done anything he suggests. Also, I'll now start having annual physicals. We will just have to work it into our budget. I want to live to be very old, and I'm not as young as I used to be, so I'll let doctors watch over my body, even though I object basically.

(4) When I left, no one had been better cared for during the past seventeen years. Well, it was back to bachelorhood. Heaven forbid! This part I feel great satisfaction over but not enough to want to continue it on shore. With my stores on board I've managed very well. I can really get around the galley and whip up a fine meal to tickle my palate. I believe I could keep Fran well fed. I've certainly had variety. Praise my wife for knowing just what to put aboard. I haven't hurt for a thing, and I'm very proud of how I manage the stove. Also, in a day, I think I've eaten a balanced diet. Washing dishes, cleaning up the slop jar, etc., has not proved to be as bad as I feared. So far, so good. I don't believe I'd like it forever, but I could do it with a smile at sea if I were part of a crew and had these duties once in a while. I'm now quite prepared to carry out the garbage each day and help with the

dishes when necessary. Fran can hold me to the last statement. I won't mind one bit.

So far I've been very pleased with my navigation. We will see how my landfall goes, but I really enjoy it. The heavenly bodies and I are getting along just fine. All the work done at home instilled confidence in my navigation, and I hope it proves not ill-founded. Shipping lanes, etc., are all where they are supposed to be according to my navigation. Radio stations also confirm it. When I get BBC on AM, I twist the antenna around, and sure enough, it's ahead. Then the sun passes my longitude right on time—a great feeling of accomplishment. This trip has been a learning and verification experience for me, one I'll never forget.

I expect the next few days to be less leisurely due to shipping and closing land. With a little luck, it should all go well. I plan to be very careful. I won't let down until *Folly* is properly moored.

Well, it's now 1515, and I have writer's cramp. And I've got a little work to do before dark.

1950   Had to refill the stove two-thirds of the way through dinner. The stove is almost full, and I finished the first gallon of alcohol. I'll have used about a gallon and a third, and I've used the stove all I wanted or needed. We will have plenty for England. After cooking pancakes, I made some drop biscuits—same utensils needed, fewer dishes to wash. Good planning. They are cooking on the stove now. I ate about eight pancakes with syrup and Ovaltine. I now have pancakes, drop biscuits, and rice all cooked and ready to eat. That should last three days or so. I've almost used one half gallon of Bisquick. I got another half gallon out of port bunk the other day. The galley isn't bad. It's just a matter of organization. I manage to get it all organized before I begin so I don't have to reach over a hot stove. This is the first time I've run out of alcohol while cooking. It lasted seven days since the last fill-up. Not bad. Maybe just one more fill-up before

Plymouth. A tee-niny breeze is coming up now. If we ignore it, I'll have wind soon.

I miss you, Fran, but I'll see you soon, with a little luck.

Fran's Log:
According to one of my two methods of calculating your progress, you could get to Plymouth as early as this Sunday. That's funny because in Beau's last article about you in the *Atlanta Constitution,* speculating about your possible position, he quoted Stuart Woods, who singlehanded the Atlantic last summer, as saying you could get there this Monday. If I had thought of all that earlier, I'd have gotten our travelers' checks today. I'll get them Monday morning so that will be taken care of.

Now I feel as if I'll hear from you soon, and that's good. All sorts of things could have happened to delay you, and I'm prepared to wait a while longer, but I'm getting excited about hearing from you. Reading and crocheting and walking the beach are about the only things I'm good for right now. If it takes you much longer, I might clean the yard, but I haven't reached that degree of desperation yet.

I have all my stuff organized so I could be ready to board a plane in thirty minutes. I'm going to be very happy and very pleased and proud of both of us when you get to Plymouth. And truly happy that you will have had a chance to make this voyage. But this isn't the way I want to spend a lot of my life.

DAY 36: *SATURDAY, JULY 16*

Log:
Noon position 48°39'.8N, 19°40'W. Day's run 56⅓.

0200   Wind freshening a little. We are starting to move along steadily. About to have tea and drop biscuit. Will stay up a while longer and sleep some during daylight hours because of shipping lanes.

0300   Will get ready for bed. Light starts about 0400 so I guess it's OK to sleep now. I might get six hours tonight and sleep a little after lunch. Will alter course when I get up. I can hear a tern outside. Maybe he will keep watch for me. Lights are all burning.

1025   I woke up at 0715. Well, it's been five weeks. I just celebrated with best breakfast yet. Grits with bacon chips, two scrambled eggs with salt, pepper, red hot sauce, and parsley flakes. I heated two biscuits with the eggs and put some margarine on them. Then I had a glass of hot tea. I had a can of apple juice when I got up. I'm getting quite a few dishes to wash. Wish we had salt water in the galley.

1226   At 1223 the sun peeked through the cloud cover and I got a shot. No filter needed. The wind is shifting more westerly. I worked my morning shot, and all is well. Waves are beginning to make up a little.

1250   635 to Plymouth. Sunshine in England. We are moving right along. Listening to Benson & Hedges cricket match and a horse race.

1330   Just had a pod of pilot whales go by. I shot eleven or twelve pictures. Also one shot of a shearwater. I have now shot about three and one-half rolls of film. This is the second pod of pilot whales this trip. This group stayed about 25 to 30 minutes and then they just disappeared.

1630   I've done the dishes. New routine worked very well. I put a bucket of salt water just outside the companionway and washed the dishes in that. It was easier and I didn't have to leave the cabin and worry about a wave breaking over me.

I'm celebrating five weeks at sea. Who knows? I could be in Plymouth next weekend. Only time will tell.

2010   After dinner the sails backed and the self-steerer disengaged. I quickly put on foul weather gear and harness and went out and put her back on course and engaged the gear. I think that's the second or third time it's happened on the trip. I hope I don't have to do that again tonight. The boat tracked downwind for a little while when I was putting on my foul weather gear to go on deck, and I was surprised. This thing just about ran downwind by herself. Then she backed, but we didn't heel over too much. She hove to pretty well. We are doing about 6½ knots. Really moving and in the right direction. I should have a good day's run tomorrow.

Tape:

2030. I'm taping earlier tonight because the weather is a little rough. I'm having an after-dinner peach brandy for a work reward. I hadn't had any on the trip, and it just dawned on me that I had some aboard, so I thought, what the heck, other singlehanders talk about coming in and having their whisky and tea, or whatever they mix, so I came in and had some peach brandy.

I was hoping the front would pass during the day, but it's still coming, and it clouded over again. It was dry during the day, but it got wet this evening. This could be the front that went through New York and knocked out the power. Maybe it will all blow over by the time I get to England, and I'll have nice weather in the Channel.

This could get worse before it gets better. I think I've had my three storms now. Don't need another one.

Fran's Log:

I got a nice letter from Beau today along with two pictures, a copy of his latest article, and a copy of a letter that Governor Busbee is sending to Ambassador Kingman Brewster. We're supposed to call him when we get to England.

I think you are probably in or near the most dangerous part of the voyage now, so be careful.

DAY 37: *SUNDAY, JULY 17*

Log:

Noon position 48°56′N, 16°11′.5W. Day's run 136.

0920   I woke up at 0730 and got up. It's a bit cooler. I get frost
from my breath in the cabin. Real North Atlantic
weather. It's very overcast. It will be damp and cold today. I'll stay in foul weather gear. It's more comfortable. I
just put on my white wool socks and powdered my feet
and boots with BFI. It feels good.

This weather reminds me of some Boy Scout trips when I
was a teenager. It's like huddling in a pup tent, trying to
keep out the elements, wind and rain. There was always a
tinge of adventure in camping out, even when it was in
the backyard. Well, I'm not in the backyard, but I'm not
a little boy anymore. Or am I? Look at the price of my
toys. Beats model railroading a little.

I feel rested and can be a little sentimental today. It is
Sunday. I've come a long way since I was a teenager.
Among my peers as a child, you would never have picked
me to do something like this. I'm sure many people back
home say, "Not Eddie!" when they hear of what I'm doing. I guess there is something to the saying, "The weaker
survive." I feel so young. When I see friends, I'm always
struck dumbfounded by the way they have aged, physically and mentally. I guess I never grew up. And I'd
prefer not to. I can't always realize that at forty-one I
could have children in their twenties.

I know my parents can't always understand what pos-
sesses me to walk to the beat of a different drummer. But
I am what I am because of them, not in spite of them.
The most important thing was that they never broke my
spirit. They instilled in me the belief that with hard work
and perseverance I could do anything. They were right.

I have enough tequila left for one more light one. Well,
I'm almost there, so it's all right if I run out of tequila.
I'm celebrating tonight. I seem to be celebrating every

night. I'll not be able to when I close the coast so I'd better now. I'll tape after a while. I've got the recorder out. Sure was a good dinner. I'm pleasingly full. The wind has freshened a little. Hope Jake copes with it through the night. I'll help if he needs me. I changed radio batteries tonight.

Tape:

2300. We're bounding along on a port running reach, almost downwind, doing about 130°. I think the low is beginning to turn me loose and the barometer is beginning to rise. All around England it's falling. The weather that just passed me is hitting the English coast now, but I still have some wind, as you can hear outside. For a few hours they will have gale force winds along the South Coast. Maybe when I get to the Channel, we'll be between lows and have some good weather. We had some big, long, rolling waves from the west today instead of choppy ones. I guess this is typical North Atlantic weather.

The first roll of charts I took out of the net was the right one. I got them out to study the approaches. I have a large-scale chart of the Scilly Isles that I'll get onto in a couple of days. Then I have one from the Lizard over to Plymouth, an approach chart into Plymouth, and a large-scale chart of Plymouth. I also have charts of Falmouth in case anything happens. I'll go around the Eddystone Rocks and on into Plymouth. It doesn't look bad at all. I've been poring over those charts, and I've read a bit already in *Reed's Nautical Almanac.* I'll get out the sailing directions, and I'll be in good shape. I'll have to start keeping track of the tides, too.

I marked on the chart I'm navigating on where the first full-scale chart of the Channel begins so I'll know when to go over onto it. I was pleased to see that those charts cover more area and come out farther than I thought. After I get onto that chart, it will be more a matter of coastal navigation. There are several buoys out there that I'll be able to sail to. I'll skirt the Scilly Isles by a good margin. I don't want to get up close to those things. It will add a little distance to the trip, but I'd rather add a little distance than get into trouble. I don't have any auxiliary power so I'll stay away from land. I don't know when I'll spot land. I might see the shore before I get to Plymouth. I don't know how high the land is. I've been familiarizing myself with all the information on the charts. They are very graphic and well laid out and give you plenty of information, especially about currents, which American charts don't on a regular navigational chart. You have to get pilot charts for that. I have the marina marked on all my charts. I did that at home.

I'm getting more and more excited knowing we're going to be together soon. I don't know how many more days at sea I'll have—five or six unless I have some calm days. I could be in Friday night or Saturday. Anyway, by the weekend you should know.

DAY 38: *MONDAY, JULY 18*

Log:

Noon position 48°47′.9N, 14°07′.5W. Day's run 98.

0930   I got up at 0700. The sun was out so I went out and took a sun shot at 0800, which is really 0900. I'm in Greenwich Time Zone now. I'll change at noon. I made the last time zone! Isn't that great! I then worked out my sun shot.

I'm 320 from Scilly Isles and 415 from Plymouth. May be there Saturday. Our heading is 90°. The wind is backing. That's the heading I want. I'll be south of my great circle, but I wanted to avoid some of the very shallow spots around the Great Sole Bank. I'll get out sailing directions sometime today. Two days and I'll be on the large-scale chart of the English Channel. Wish you were here this moment, Fran, with warm clothes to wear. We will get your Atlantis foul weather gear next. It's good.

1500   I've gone on Greenwich Time. I went out an hour too early for my noon shot. I kept shooting and wondering why the degrees kept getting higher and higher. The sun was supposed to come over me at 1145. But it was 1045. I had misread my watch. I went back out at 1145 and got my noon shot.

1955   I haven't seen any ships today so I'm celebrating Edison's

Day. One hundred years ago today the phonograph was invented. BBC is a wealth of information. I'm listening to barbershop quartet music and really enjoying it.

Tape:
Midnight. When I get to Plymouth, I'll call you first and then I'll call Mom and Dad. I'm sure they're going to want to know that I've gotten in safely. Then I'll call Beau. On a weekend I probably won't be able to catch him. He'll be out at the lake.

I've cruised over here; I haven't raced. I've made good time, but if I were racing I would be a lot more careful and do a lot more sail changing. I could cut a good bit of time off this trip. With reachers and spinnakers I would have averaged more miles a day. I'm averaging one hundred miles a day over the ground still. I'm getting where I'm going in a nice, professional, safe manner. We're sure trying to do that.

Fran's Log:
After lunch I went to the bank and got our travelers' checks. If I heard from you after 1:30 in the afternoon or on a weekend and could get a flight out right away, I'd hate to have to wait for a bank to open before I could do anything.

DAY 39: *TUESDAY, JULY 19*

Log:
Noon position 49°02'.1N, 11°55'W. Day's run 99¾.

1105   We are about 230 nautical miles from Scilly Isles and 325 from Plymouth. Getting anxious. We are on a port reach now. Moving right along. I should be on a large-scale chart tomorrow. I got a morning sun shot and might get noon shot.

1210   I'm ready for a landfall now. I shaved and spruced up. Then I went out and reset the log. I came in and put on long john bottoms and an LSU sweatshirt. I don't know where that came from. It fits. If I can stay dry, I'll come in

like this. I retired my red and white pajamas and green
sweater to the dirty clothes bag.

2100   I've worked out high and low tides for Plymouth. They
look good for coming in during the morning. It also looks
like good weather if I can believe the radio. Even warm-
ing a little. The tides won't be running at their highest—
18 feet. Instead, they'll just be a mean 15 feet. Ha! Everything looks good so far.

2120   Felt the need for dessert. Got out pineapple chunks.
Going to enjoy it now. I'm eating like a horse. If I'm not
careful, I'll get fat. I'm at that age, you know.

2200   Looked around. All is well. The stars are bright between
scattered clouds. The sky looks different up here. Big
Dipper is very high in the sky. I'll rest a little now.

Tape:

Midnight.   As of right now, there are five ships all around.
All day long there was nothing. Three hours ago, nothing. About
an hour ago it was the strangest thing. I had just gotten out of
my foul weather gear and stretched out on my bunk. It was so
relaxing. I had the self-steerer set. It looked as if the boat had
gone over on another tack, so I got up to check.

I looked out and there were five boats. I took the helm for a
little while, and the bow light blew out. I have a little battery
power yet, so I turned on running lights. I was pretty close to
some of those ships. I got the bow light, brought it back and relit
it, and went back up to the bow and put it in the bracket. I hope
it burns all night. I might have had it too low, but when it is too
high, it gets sooty. Thank God it's nice out.

This is either a large fishing fleet or NATO forces on maneuvers. I heard that NATO ships were maneuvering southwest of
England, and that's where I am. I think I'll get by them all pretty
easy. We're doing our 90°. Boy, am I back to civilization now! I
figured by tomorrow night it would be like this. No sleep tonight. Back to work. Is this a surprise!

The ships aren't moving very fast. It could be a fishing fleet.
They aren't tankers. Tankers would already have gone by. They
aren't freighters because they are all lit up. I was afraid they
might be tow barges, but they aren't towing anything. They are

leaving me alone and letting me get on by and get out of their way, and that's good. That's what I want to do—just get out of their way. I don't want them to get upset with me. They might have wondered what I was, especially with that bow light blown out.

If this is a fishing fleet, some of the boats are big processing boats, and smaller boats are running around. They could be Russian or Norwegian. They are supposed to be outside the two-hundred-mile limit, because they've hauled a boat in for fishing for cod inside the limit. But they aren't out much farther than that because we're within two hundred miles of the English coast now. No need to try to figure it out. I won't be able to see them in the morning. They'll be gone, and I'll be left out here all by myself again. I have my flags flying to report me to Lloyd's if anybody sees me while I'm sleeping. If I talk to anybody, I'll give them your phone number and have them call you.

I just looked out again. I'm heading east and they are heading north. For a while I thought they were trying to hem me in and look me over. I had one off to port for a while and one off to starboard, and it looked as if I couldn't get away from them. Finally I fell off behind the one to starboard. It's interesting. I expect the Channel to be like this—loaded with ships. I'll really have to watch. I have the two cabin lamps burning; the bow light and stern light are on. I have the curtains pulled to let as much light out as possible. We'll just have to go with that. I have no power to move away from them except sail power. As long as I have wind, I can move a little. If they catch me when the wind is down, I'll just have to shine lights or something. But they aren't that close to me now. I'm doing all right.

Everything is verifying that I'm closing the coast. My navigation must be pretty close. The wave action is different now—rougher. I came over the eight-hundred-fathom curve, and I'll be getting into shallower water than that. There's a place that has seven fathoms that I wanted to stay south of. I was a few miles south of it, and when I was in that area, I swear to you the waves looked bigger. It's little things like that that verify my navigation. I managed to by-pass all the shallow spots that were on my great circle. There were a couple of places that shallowed out, so I went quite a way west of them.

Let me check outside one more time. My bow light is still lit. It looks as if there's a double row of ships in a line going north. I'll just have to check every so often and hold my course. I'm still doing 90°. These boats are working the coast. They aren't going toward it.

I ought to be in directly. Shouldn't be too long.

DAY 40: *WEDNESDAY, JULY 20*

Log:

Noon position 49°26′.2N, 09°08′W. Day's run 145¼.

0200   All clear. Rest one hour.

0300   Two ships—one port and one starboard.

0340   Boat crossed bow. I helped steer around her. Both boats to starboard now. Bow light blown out. Had a glass of hot tea. I have cozy green gloves on. I'm glad the decks are dry tonight. Jake doing a good job. These must be fishing boats. They are big.

1415   I studied the large-scale chart some more, and I'm now on it. You can see the color of the water changing. It's greenish. Haven't seen any boats today. I'll try to nap a little.

1950   We were about 110 miles from the Scilly Isles at noon. Hope they show up in the morning. I got out sailing directions and read them. They were the first ones in the top of the cabinet. I just might see some lights early in the morning. The weather is beautiful and is supposed to be good tomorrow.

2030   No ships on the horizon. It's just sunset now. I pumped the bilge today—about a gallon or so—not bad. I'll relax a little now.

2140   It's getting dark. All lights are burning and the stars are coming out. It's beautiful. Cygnus is just about overhead. I look north and I realize I'm looking at stars I've never seen before. The North Star and Big Dipper are high in the sky. I'm listening to Jascha Heifetz playing violin on Radio 4. Just had a hot tea with Courvoisier and feel nice and warm. No lights on the horizon. All is well. Almost like a dream world. I'm about seventy miles offshore now. Maybe with a little luck I'll see lights in the morning sky. I'll rest now. This is as pretty a night as we have had on the trip.

2400   Eating fruit cocktail and taping.

Tape:

0030 (7/21).   At 2220 I heard what sounded like a double explosion outside—as if somebody was firing on me. I hopped out of the bunk. I could hear a jet plane afterward. I think it broke the sound barrier in my area.

The weather reports are all good, with good wind for the rig that I have up. And it's supposed to be dry for the most part—maybe a shower or two. Around noon I could be off the Scilly Isles. I'll have to go north some to get in close to them. About 0800 if I haven't noticed anything, I'll alter more to the north. I'm traveling more east now, and I'll point up more northeast. I just wanted to be sure I would come in south of those islands.

I hope you sleep well tonight. I'm going to meditate real hard about being so close. Maybe you'll get the vibrations. I wonder how your past forty days have gone. It's hard to look back now and realize it's been that long, but that's what it's been—forty days of water and weather. The end of the trip looks as if it's treating me pretty well.

The boats I saw last night were over banks where it shallows up. I guess they fish there. I don't know what sort of fish they were after. I haven't noticed any particular fish life in the area, but I haven't spent a lot of time out in the cockpit looking over the side.

The ride is different over this shallow water. It's a different feel when you come in over the hundred-fathom curve. Now I think we're in less than a hundred fathoms of water. The wind is force 2 or 3, but we're moving along pretty well. I had registered thirty-six miles by 1800, and that was just a six-hour run. I didn't think the boat was going that fast, but that's what the log said, and the log is supposed to be right. We're not due to be becalmed out here, but you never know. The weatherman isn't sitting out here.

Tomorrow night I might see the Eddystone Lighthouse. I

don't know if I'll see the lighthouse on Bishop's Rock. There's an outside chance I might see some rays from it by daybreak. It only shows for twenty-some miles. I won't be surprised if I don't see it. I'd like to be close enough to see the coast tomorrow. I just don't know what to expect but when I see it, I'll know it. Some of the countryside is supposed to be kind of high and hilly so I guess I could see it from a good way off.

I still have the flags flying, but I don't know that they'll do any good. I'll be in the English Channel before anybody sees me, I guess. After a boat or two has seen them, I'll probably take them down and put up the British ensign.

Traffic will get a little heavier. I'll keep all my lights burning and try to stay out of everybody's way. It was nice last night to see life around me again and to know they weren't out in the middle of the Atlantic playing around. Their fishing banks come out farther than they do in the United States, where the continental shelf drops off a lot sooner. Sixty miles and you're out in the Gulf Stream. You can fish there but not much farther out.

I'm lucky to have good weather.

Fran's Log:
Today I did a lot of manual labor and it was very therapeutic. At least I'm now so tired I don't have the energy to be anything but relaxed. I didn't do it for its therapeutic value. I did it from necessity. When they pave the driveway, the only way we can get out of the house is through the front door next to the shower door and around the north side of the house. There's no cactus on the north side, but the weeds were waist high. I took the swing blade and started hacking away. I cleared it in four sessions—two this morning and two this afternoon. Now it's passable.

I started reading *Walden* today. I should have read it long ago, but maybe it wouldn't have meant the same things to me.

I want you to be as close to Plymouth as I think you are. If so, someone should see you and report you or I should hear from you soon. I can't do anything except feel certain that you're all right and almost there.

DAY 41: *THURSDAY, JULY 21*

Log:

Noon position 49°34'N, 6°51'W. Day's run 105½.

0300   One ship to port and one to starboard. Just woke up. Ships are quite a way ahead of me. No other lights.

0815   Wind switched to southwest. Starboard running reach. Traveler bearing just broke. One of the little pins on the center part that slides across broke off. Lost sheave. Jury rigged with sail ties.

0905   Just made permanent repairs to traveler. Had a screw that fit. Also cut more sail ties.

0925   Just saw the top of a fishing boat heading south. My first one in daylight hours.

1430   I just fixed the traveler again. I hope it holds now. I got a noon shot and morning shot. I am having to head more northerly to make my landfall. I'll know by sunset. Making a landfall is a little nerve-wracking.

Several ships have come across my bow. Then some head east and others go south. Can't pick up anything on RDF. It's on the blink, I guess. I was afraid of that before I left. Well, Columbus didn't have an RDF.

1712   Big sloop heading southeast off starboard bow 5 or 6 miles away. It must be heading toward the French coast. I just had dinner—ravioli, cookies, and cold tea. A light Courvoisier and soda. A jet just broke the sound barrier again. A big freighter passed me to port. I couldn't see it long. It's raining lightly. It will be dark soon. I'm heading in the right direction.

Tape:

0400 (7/22).   It's midnight your time.

All day today I sat out in the cockpit. I didn't catch any lights last night. I was hoping to see Bishop's Rock way off, but no such luck. Tonight we've had rain and fog.

After it got dark, about a dozen trawlers went by on either side of me. I went right down the middle of them. The last one was working when I came up on it, and I had to help the boat, or it would have run me down. I don't think they saw me. These trawlers are a pretty good size.

Just keep our fingers crossed and say a little prayer that we're on target. I hope the sextant is OK. I've worked out the shots the best I can. I'm going to set the course toward Eddystone Lighthouse as if I've been doing this all my life and see if we end up in that area. I don't know how far you can see Lizard if the fog lifts. This has got to be the Channel with all this fog. Anyway, I'm not losing heart yet. If I get lost out here, I'll have to ask directions. So far, so good. I haven't run into any rocks or another boat.

As far as talking to a ship out here, I'd have to raise a really big ruckus because they go around. All the ships I've seen so far, fishing boats or anything else, have stayed away except for that one last night. It would have run me down if I had been sleeping. I don't know if they were pulling nets, or what. I wouldn't want to be behind them. I went through a lot of fishing ground yesterday. There was a lot of twine in the water. The fishermen just cut twine loose and leave it in the water.

I've got the tides and currents in the sailing directions and everything else, and I've been keeping track of everything the best I can. The currents are sketched out nicely in the sailing directions so I can see how they shift. I'm going to add a little bit—or what I think is a little bit—for a margin of safety before I make my turn in to head closer to land. It will be daylight, and maybe this fog will burn off. Let's hope it does. It's supposed to be just patch fog. If it burns off by 0800 or 1000, maybe I'll come up just where I should and see the Lizard off my port bow, but of course I'll be heading more northeast then. I'll have to change over to about 70° to run on in toward Eddystone. Or that's what I *think* I'm going to be heading toward. We'll see how close the sextant shots have been. It's just awfully foggy right now, but I don't hear any ships or foghorns around. I should be south of the inbound lane, and I expect everything is spaced all right. Traffic may not be too heavy there. We'll see.

Fran's Log:

Well, I guess everybody is getting antsy. Joe Caldwell called today and said the wire services had been calling him asking if we had heard any news. I told him I will call when I hear, of course. I also told him that you should be getting close.

Then Beau called. He speculates that you could be three hundred miles out now. I told him that puts you in the middle between my two methods of plotting, so that seemed fair.

Beau had called Lloyd's. They told him that they hadn't had any reports, but that they could well get a few as you get close to England. They had a note in their file to call Malvina. Beau also called the British Coast Guard at Land's End. They hadn't had any reports but suggested that someone at the Royal Western Yacht Club in Plymouth might also get a report. Beau will call and check with them. With all that and the governor's suggestion to Ambassador Brewster that he alert the RAF, Beau figures he has spread a good network over the area.

Beau's other news was that the weather west of England is deteriorating. I had thought that it was, based on the little I could see on the TV weather map. He said there is a storm system four hundred miles southeast of Greenland with average winds up to thirty knots. It's moving down and the ocean west of England has winds twenty to thirty knots with eight- to twelve-foot seas and gusts to forty knots in squalls. I could wish you had had weather like that farther out instead of closing land when you'll need more and better sextant shots instead of fewer and worse or none at all.

I told Beau that I felt this was the most dangerous part of the voyage—closing an unfamiliar coast—but that I was sure you would do it wisely. I'll just be so happy to know you're there and are all right. I want to be with you.

DAY 42: *FRIDAY, JULY 22*

Log:

Noon position 49°30′N, 05°08′.5W. Day's run 97.

0750   I changed course to Eddystone area. Hope the sextant was right yesterday. No sign of coast yet except very thick fog (due all day) and foghorns of boats north of me. Sure wish I could have seen Land's End or Lizard. I'm on

D.R. There won't be any sun shots today. Well, here's hoping.

Recollection:

On my last days at sea I was too busy to tape. After breakfast the fog lifted somewhat in that we would sail into clear areas. I could hear the sound of diesels from fishing boats heading in my direction. I was using my foghorn. They would come almost to a dead stop in the water some distance away and then alter course and go around me. The shipping lanes for large shipping were north of me. This was verified every once in a while by their foghorns.

At noon it had been too overcast all day to get any shots. I sailed into a clear area and spotted a French fishing boat about thirty-five to forty feet long. They seemed to be working a "throw line" as we refer to them in Louisiana—a long line that could be buoyed with baited hooks. They were not trolling. I sailed into their area and got their attention. By about 1230 they had motored up to my position. No one aboard spoke English, and in my broken French I was trying to get a heading from them for either Plymouth or Eddystone Light. He indicated that I was headed on the right course and what I took in conversation to be some thirty-plus miles from Plymouth. After this he went back to his work.

I consulted the chart and was quite sure, after looking at it, that he meant some forty-odd miles southwest of Eddystone Lighthouse. As my French is very poor, I would not be surprised if the mixup was totally mine.

Looking over the stern, I saw what appeared to be either a fishing boat with a very high mast or a sailboat with the sails down. We were making only a couple of knots, and she seemed to be trying to catch up with me. I let off on what sail I had and waited. As she caught up with me, I found, much to my surprise, human beings who could speak my language. Needless to say, I was excited. It was a dark-hulled sloop about thirty-five to forty feet long. Aboard were a man and a woman around thirty years of age. They were from Australia and were eighteen days out of the Azores. They were under power, charging their batteries.

I explained that I was forty days out of Florida. He asked if I had gotten a position from the fishing boat. I said that my French was limited, but that I was heading for Plymouth and was on the right course and estimated I was about forty to forty-five miles southwest of Eddystone Lighthouse, but I had not been able to get sun shots for a couple of days. He told me he was en route to Falmouth. At this point he made an attempt to get a sun shot, but it was impossible with the total cloud cover. He said he had his position as 49°55′N, 5°W. I gave him my noon position of 49°30′N, 5°08′W. Since it was now about 1400, our figures were close enough so that he said he would now head due north under power for Falmouth. I went back to 65° instead of 70°. Then I decided to stick with 70°, and I continued northeast for Eddystone. The last I saw of them they were merrily motoring off into the fog.

I believe this was my most exciting moment thus far involving meeting another human being. They could speak my language, and I had an insatiable urge to swim over to their boat and shake his hand and hug his girl. The thought that kept going through my mind was, "He has a girl aboard and everything!"

After the incident I found it very strange that I had not had this urge on the two occasions when I had met people who could not speak English. All the way over on CBC I had heard discussions about the separation of Quebec from Canada and the arguments about language—English and French. Now I had come to the realization that language is the first thing that really binds human beings together. It would have been hard to convince me before this episode that that would be the case.

At about 2300 I picked up a light to the east of me and watched it carefully. It was not shipping, and I altered course to make toward it. By midnight I made out blinking amber lights below a white light maybe a hundred feet off the water, and I could also see the lights of what seemed to be a small boat moving away from this lighted object and returning to it.

No sleep tonight.

Fran's Log:

If the segments on the second part of your course are really ninety-five miles, you should get to Plymouth tomorrow. My perceptions of the usual beach pleasures are dulled. I also have to use a lot of self-control to stay civil to everybody.

DAY 43: *SATURDAY, JULY 23*

Log:

Noon position 49°40′N, 04°11′W. Day's run 90.
1000   Gale force winds. Going to Sark. Sheltered holding ground. Strong winds and building.

Recollection:

Between the hours of 0500 and 0600 I was able to determine that the lights were emanating from a metal tower that was not on my charts. By 0800 I had gotten close enough to identify the tower as an oil rig on a concrete base with what we in Louisiana refer to as a "crew boat" anchored off its northeast point. I sailed due north of this structure and about this time started getting bulletins from the BBC that we were due for gale force conditions. The weather had been deteriorating.

Having had no sleep in over twenty-four hours and being aware of the shipping lanes north of me and aware of the fact that I might get into the Eddystone area during a northerly gale, I reevaluated my plans. After careful examination of the chart and after reading the sailing directions and all the information available, I decided to seek shelter behind the island of Sark, which I could make by early morning. My greatest problem at the moment was finding a British possession on the south side of the Channel. I was, after all, carrying a gift and a proclamation for the Queen of England.

I knew that I would not get any more rest and did not feel safe enough to lie ahull or heave to in the Channel with all the shipping around. I also knew quite well the characteristics and manageability of my boat running before a gale, so I altered course. Southeast of Sark I could get in the lee of the island and find four fathoms of water or less to anchor until the gale abated or I could get a tow into port.

Between the hours of 1600 and 2200 I went through the south-west-bound and northeast-bound shipping lanes. After clearing the shipping lanes, I took out my anchor and four hundred feet of rope and lashed them on deck. By nightfall I was getting into a position to alter course due east and head for Sark. There was a possibility that I could have picked up the Guernsey lighthouse, but because of squalls and very poor visibility, I didn't. I spent most of the time in the cockpit handling the boat myself while going through the heavy traffic, which I managed very well, crossing at about a 90° angle.

Before midnight there were two big happenings. Just before sunset I decided to have a can of peaches and a cup of tea. It was my habit to open a can of peaches a quarter of the way and drink the fluid, then open it all the way and eat the peaches. This kept me from spilling the liquid all over my beard on a bounding boat. I had just finished drinking the fluid when the sails needed my attention on deck. I went topside and retrimmed the sails.

When I came back into the cabin, I lit the stove and was boiling water for tea when I looked over my shoulder and saw the peaches sitting on the table opened only a quarter of the way. I was seized with the only feeling of split personality I experienced on the entire trip. My mind reasoned that the captain had started to open the peaches and had not completed the job. Here I was, the galley slave, carrying this free-loader all the way across the ocean. I said very loudly, "Aw shit! Just once couldn't you have opened the peaches?" All this took about thirty seconds, and when I realized what I had thought and said, I had an uproarious laugh at myself.

Just before midnight the boat was really being tossed around in fairly high winds. I felt a little damp and chilly so I decided to have a cup of hot tea. I opened the valve slightly on the right-hand burner for a few seconds and then shut it off. I took a match and placed it close to the alcohol in the cup under the stove. Instantly a small portion of the counter top lit up with the burner. There was also a potholder under the stove whose surface was lit. I reached for a bottle of water we keep handy in the sink for just this purpose and instinctively reached for the potholder under the stove. As I did this, alcohol spilled on the top of my hand from the burner in a beautiful blue glow. I withdrew my flaming hand and potholder, doused them quickly with water, and also doused the top of the counter. The only casualties were a few singed hairs on my hand and a scorched potholder, which I threw out into the cockpit in a rage.

I had left the burner slightly open after my peaches and tea an hour or so earlier. It was the first and last time I will ever leave a burner ajar. We were careful always to keep water close at hand, and for myself, I was exceedingly happy that it was alcohol and not flaming kerosene. I will say that the tea was quite fine after the water boiled. I attribute this incident partly to my being overly fatigued.

Fran's Log:

Little worries try to tug at my brain, and I won't let myself consider them. I just read and walk the beach and look forward to seeing you.

DAY 44: *SUNDAY, JULY 24*

Log:

Day's run 81¼.

Recollection:

I was expecting to pick up the lighthouse of Sark north of me in the early morning hours if my dead reckoning was correct. We were in gale force winds. The going was very wet and rough, and my feet felt chilled from either perspiration or water that had seeped into my boots. I went below quickly and got a dry pair of wool socks from the top of my winter clothes bag. I slipped them on and they took care of my cold-foot problem immediately.

On coming out of the cabin—this was approximately 0200—I looked off to port and saw the blink of a light. I reached into my foul weather jacket pocket, pulled out my stopwatch, and timed the light. Sure enough. There was Sark.

It was pitch black out, and I saw no other lights in the area. I altered course and headed the light. As I closed the coast, the seas and winds abated. At about 0330 I began noticing that the light sometimes disappeared so that I could see only its rays. Then I realized there were very large, high rocks between me and it.

I worked my way around until I could see the light again and tacked back and forth, waiting for daylight. After 0400, with the first light of dawn, I found myself among partially submerged rocks, and the large rocks that had gotten between me and the lighthouse were now south-southwest of me. I was almost clear of the rocks when the keel struck. I hung onto the tiller and the boat drove over the submerged rocks, heeling at about 40° plus. As the keel cleared, the rudder struck. I was now faced with a steering casualty. The tiller would move freely to port but would stop amidship and not budge to starboard. I immediately lashed the tiller amidship and steered by using the two lines from the self-steering vane, whose rudder submerges about ten inches in the water and had not been damaged. The log was fouled in the self-steering rudder, but I quickly cleared it and brought it aboard fairly knotted up. I sailed along the coast until I was clear of all rocks and abreast of the lighthouse three-quarters of a mile to a mile offshore. By 0500 I had dropped all sails and lay ahull.

At about 0515 two boats sailed out of Sark and one came within hailing distance of me. It was a dark-colored hull, ketch-rigged, thirty-five to forty feet long. Aboard were a man in his fifties and a younger woman. They made a complete circle around my boat while I explained my position and asked for a tow. He refused. I then asked him to go back to Sark and ask any motor launch to come out and give me a tow into port. He refused and sailed away. I couldn't believe it. I don't think I have ever been so stunned.

I then drank a can of grapefruit juice and thought about what I should do next. Since the weather looked fairly clear and the seas were fairly smooth, I thought I would try to anchor where I was. I lowered the anchor over thirty feet without touching bottom and hauled it back aboard. At about 0600 I took out my 37-mm flare gun and fired two flares, hoping to attract attention from the lighthouse. Fog was making up over the island, and I got no response. I then got my international code book and looked up proper flags to fly from the spreader for assistance. By

0630 I had hoisted these flags, turned the American ensign upside down, and cut two large orange flags from a lifejacket. I flew one from the flag halyard and one from the backstay. By the time I had completed this, it was about 0800, and I had drifted a distance of two and a half or three miles south of the island.

Next I began to experiment with different sail combinations so that I could tack against the wind with a fair amount of control with my self-steering rudder. I found that I could do pretty well with reefed main and storm jib. About 1030 I sailed up in the vicinity of a twenty-four- or twenty-five-foot sailboat and tried to attract their attention by waving my arms above my head. I got no response. I fired one parachute flare and got an immediate response. The boat approached me. She was the *Beg-Lem* from Ecole de voile du Chateau du Taureau in St. Malo. Aboard were two sailing instructors with their French sailing students. One spoke English. He was put aboard *Folly* with me, and we sailed for about thirty minutes to a good holding ground and dropped the anchor.

We took down all signs of distress, left the British ensign flying with the "Q" flag on the starboard flag halyard, and the American ensign right-side-up on the backstay. The French boat had no engine, so a tow into port was impossible. The instructor said it was too dangerous to sail into Sark, and they assured me my boat would be quite safe while they took me to Jersey, their next port of call, where I could arrange for a tow.

The French crew were very kind and gave me French bread, fine cheese, and French wine for my very first meal in my new world. How relaxing it was to be a passenger again. I must have looked pretty tired as they made every effort to make me comfortable and tried to get me to sleep. I managed about thirty minutes to an hour on our trip to Jersey.

Upon arriving in Jersey, I had to climb a steel ladder up the side of the quay for about thirty or forty feet. I negotiated this very well, much to my surprise. At my request, Heiko Hulsker, who spoke English, dug up the first little bit of soil I stepped on. As we walked to the harbormaster's office, I broke the first blades of grass I approached and a small flower, smelled them, and put them in my bag.

The Port Authority very graciously arranged with the Sark Shipping Company for a tow from my anchorage to St. Peter Port. They were sending a ferry to bring passengers to Sark and could pick up *Folly* on their way back to Guernsey. After making these arrangements, the boys asked me the first thing I wanted to do when I came ashore, and I said, "Have a pint of bitter." We went directly to a pub at the harbor, and I had my pint of bitter.

I then walked to the nearest pay phone and called Fran, who was surprised to hear me and to know where I was, but she had been aware of the weather conditions, and was happy that I had made a safe port. While I am quite sure she worried about my personal safety, the first question she asked me was, "Do you still like sailing?" In my weakened condition, this surprised me, but I didn't have to think about it as I answered, "I sure do!"

After having completed the most pleasant telephone call of my life, I devoured four or five sandwiches at the pub, and we returned to the boat for a most relaxing and enjoyable evening. I managed four or five hours' broken sleep. This was something I had to get used to. For about three weeks I found it difficult to sleep for more than two hours at a stretch without waking up with the feeling that I was still on the boat.

In the early morning hours of the twenty-fifth the sailing instructor from the French sailboat escorted me to the SeaLink ferry for Guernsey, and we had an emotional farewell. It was a lovely ride. Upon arriving at Guernsey, I saw *Folly* sitting out in the harbor just as proud as ever.

When I stepped off the ferry, I approached the first policeman I saw. He recognized me immediately and directed me to the Sark Shipping Company, where I was put in the charge of Mr. R.G. Perkins. We went directly to the Port Authority, boarded *Folly*, and brought her around with a small motor launch to a pontoon in the inner harbor. I then checked in with Customs. I was cleared very easily and graciously—typical of the contacts I had made with people thus far, aside from the refusal of help off Sark. I do not believe that man could have been a Channel Islander or a British subject, but he must have been someone from somewhere else, involved in something he shouldn't have been involved in at the time.

Fran's Log:

I didn't have any trouble getting on a flight to London tomorrow, but we're on standby for a flight to Guernsey. That's exotic, all right. Seeing the Channel Islands is a treat I hadn't expected. But mostly I just want to see you. And tomorrow I'll be on my way.

A haggard Ed assures Fran he has successfully sailed the Atlantic alone. (Bob Baker, UPI photo)

PART 5

England

8

Buckingham Palace and Home

On our taxi ride from the Guernsey Airport to the Victoria Marina at St. Peter Port I felt as if I had been dropped into another world. Everything was in miniature—the cars, the roads, the houses. The gardens were miniature, too, in size, but there was nothing small about their brilliance. Before every cottage were great splashes of red, yellow, blue, pink, white, purple. And there were hydrangeas—one of the few flowers my uneducated eye could name—in shades I hadn't suspected that hydrangeas knew. The effect was dazzling, especially in my state of jet-lag.

The marina was a forest of masts. Our driver deposited us at the marina office, and I began asking questions. A dockmaster pointed out an American ensign in the middle of the forest, several pontoons away. I mentally translated "pontoon" to "floating dock," left Mother with our baggage, and began making my way toward the ensign. By the time I had reached what I thought was the proper pontoon, I had lost sight of the ensign.

A man with a nice-looking young face and a shock of white hair was coming up the ramp from the pontoon. I asked him if he could direct me to *Lormand's 2nd Folly*. In pleasantly

Together again after 44 days, Ed and Fran Lormand aboard Folly *in St. Peter Port, Guernsey, Channel Islands. (*The Guernsey Press Limited *photo)*

French-accented English he did, and as I continued down the ramp, I was aware that he was following me.

Ed was sitting in *Folly*'s cockpit talking to a man. The boats were rafted out and there were two between *Folly* and the pontoon. I think I called to Ed—or he looked up—and he scrambled over the intervening boats, and we stood on the dock hugging each other.

"We did it," Ed mumbled into my ear.

My kind guide was looking on and smiling, and the man Ed had been talking to was slowly making his way over the boats to the pontoon. He looked dejected—not in keeping with the spirit of the occasion.

While I was agreeing with Ed that we had, indeed, done it, I heard our sad-looking observer, who turned out to be Bob Baker, a newspaper reporter and good friend, mutter, "The only time I've come down here without my camera."

Ed looked good, sounded good, felt good. And since he apparently had no inclination to leave *Folly* for a night ashore, I was reassured that he still liked her and sailing. We found a pleasant guest lodge for Mother within walking distance of the marina, and I moved aboard the boat for the duration of our stay in St. Peter Port.

Folly looked good, too, and except for our homemade Bimini top and the cover for the vegetable bin that were blown to shreds, she looked none the worse for wear. She had justified our assessment of her substantial quality and that of the gear and equipment we had added.

What did that mean in terms of our future? We had prepared *Folly* and ourselves for Ed's singlehanded transatlantic voyage, and not only had it been concluded successfully, but Ed had enjoyed it. It had been everything he wanted it to be and more. Now, after forty-two days alone at sea, he still wanted to sail around the world nonstop alone. And now, more than ever before, he was convinced that he could do it. And again, those were the two basic reasons—indeed the obligation—to do anything.

On February 17, 1976, before Ed's first transatlantic attempt, I had written the following entry in my log: "People ask me, 'And you are really going to let him go?' One of the reasons I love Ed

Ed in Guernsey shortly after his arrival. (The Guernsey Press Limited *photo)*

so much is that he has the kind of imagination and spirit of adventure that make him want a trip like this. If I refused my support, it would be a denial of myself as well as of him. It is a fascinating project, and I'm enjoying it." By July 1977 I had found no reason to change my mind.

If I had really wanted to say, "No," I should have said it years ago and married someone with more conventional ambitions. Now I simply agreed to one more singlehanded voyage—around the world, nonstop—and started making the first list.

The marina at St. Peter Port was full of boats from all over the world, and Guernsey itself was full of visitors. It was the height of the tourist season, and Ed and *Folly* were local celebrities. The newspaper and radio and television reporters came for interviews and pictures, spreading the word about the lone American sailor. The policemen assigned to the marina area came down to see *Folly* when they came on duty, tipped their hats and talked to her skipper, and then directed tourists down the pontoon.

Life aboard *Folly* was a continual open house. Our visitors were other yachtsmen and their children, native Guernsey-folk, tourists, and local students, many of whom we introduced to American-style popcorn. They examined the boat, quizzed Ed about his voyage, and in turn extended their own generous hospitality. We had more invitations to visit people in England than we could squeeze into a year, much less six weeks. And they were all fascinated by Ed's gift for the Queen and the proclamation that he had brought from the governor and the people of Georgia. The Queen's Silver Jubilee had been a heartwarming occasion for Britons. All of them wanted to know about the arrangements that were being made for the presentation. Would we go to Buckingham Palace? Would the Queen see us? Would she sign Ed's logbook?

One of the children who visited aboard, the daughter of a British yachtsman who had sailed over to the Channel Islands for a family vacation, heard us discussing the possibility of going to the palace. Helen, the little girl, disappeared for a while. When she returned, she slipped an envelope into Ed's hand. Later, when everyone had gone away, we looked at it. It was a charming note addressed "To Queen," printed in pencil, telling

Ed and faithful "Jake" in Guernsey in July, 1977. Bob Baker, UPI photo)

the queen how much Helen had enjoyed the Jubilee celebrations and seeing her on television. The note was put away safely for delivery along with the gift and the proclamation.

The American Embassy's Information Office was handling the arrangements for the transfer. Our own expectations were not great. It looked as though the Queen herself would be away from London when we were likely to be there. If the gift, the proclamation, and Helen's note were picked up at the embassy by a palace messenger, it would be all right. It was important only that they be delivered appropriately and with our good wishes.

While we were enjoying making new friends and wondering how we could ever hope to repay the kind of hospitality we were receiving, we were making arrangements to lay *Folly* up in Guernsey until next summer. Mr. Perkins of the Sark Shipping Company put us in touch with the Guernsey Boatbuilding & Engineering Company. They would be able to fix the rudder and find a corner in their yard where *Folly* could stay in dry storage until next June.

August 3 was a bright, sunny day. We had packed our traveling clothes, given away what was left of the perishable food, and closed the hatch. Mr. Perkins would take care of moving *Folly* to the yard. We had a rental car waiting for us in London for a six-week tour of the mainland. And we had a gift and messages to deliver to the Queen. We promised ourselves that we would return during our month-long Christmas holiday.

In London, American Embassy personnel were working on the arrangements for us to deliver the gift. They were also scheduling newspaper and radio interviews as well as an appointment with Ambassador Kingman Brewster.

We did our London sightseeing and our interviews, and on August 9 at 5:30 we had a pleasant visit with Ambassador Brewster in his office at the embassy. A yachtsman himself, he had asked that Ed bring his charts, and the two of them spread charts over the coffee table and spent several minutes going over them and discussing the voyage. We promised the ambassador a picture of *Folly*, returned down a corridor lined with portraits of former ambassadors, and signed the guest book.

Now Ed's voyage would be complete when the gift and proc-

Ambassador Kingman Brewster, a fellow American yachtsman, and Ed going over the charts of Folly's *voyage in Ambassador Brewster's office at the American Embassy in London, August 9, 1977. (John Hammond photo)*

lamation and a little girl's note were delivered to Buckingham Palace. The appointment had been made for 12:30, Thursday, August 11. We would be received by Lt. Colonel Blair Stewart-Wilson, deputy master of the household.

The first order of that day was to find presentable clothes for Ed to wear. He had nothing but boat clothes, and he wanted to rent, not buy. All our inquiries produced the same answer— Moss Brothers. On the morning of the eleventh we presented ourselves at that establishment and explained our problem. Thirty minutes later Ed emerged looking elegant in a fine dark suit. The only things he had on that belonged to him were his socks and underwear.

Helen McCain Smith and a photographer from the embassy accompanied Ed, Mother, and me to the palace in the embassy limousine. We arrived just after the changing of the guard, and mobs of people and their automobiles were leaving the area. Helen showed a policeman her identification and said that Mr. Lormand had an appointment in the palace at 12:30. Suddenly bobbies sprang out of the pavement and cars parted like the Red Sea. We drove through the gate and inside the grounds and stopped next to a red carpet. A butler met us at the door, ushered us into a small sitting room, and went away to tell Lt. Colonel Stewart-Wilson that we were there.

In two or three minutes Colonel Stewart-Wilson came in apologizing for keeping us waiting. He seemed genuinely interested in Ed's voyage. He said that the Queen knew that we were there, that she was sorry that she couldn't be there, and that she had sent him back to the palace to meet us and accept the gift and proclamation in her behalf. The royal family were in Northern Ireland.

We knew that photographs were not allowed inside the palace. In fact, our photographer had warned us not to be alarmed if he were asked to wait outside. But no one had done that, and now Colonel Stewart-Wilson said that he knew we would like to have pictures. Instead of leading us outside, he suggested that the quadrangle would be more private. We followed him to the quadrangle, the inner courtyard of the palace.

There he gave us a mini-tour. He pointed out the Prince of Wales' door, the King's Door, and the Queen's Door onto the courtyard. He told us that the courtyard had been open until Queen Victoria's reign. She had had so many children that she needed more rooms, and the front section of the palace was added, closing the quadrangle. He stood with us for pictures while he received the gift and proclamation before the King's Door in the courtyard. He was delighted with little Helen's note and said that the Queen would be also.

Ed had a final question. Would it be proper to ask the Queen and Prince Philip to sign his logbook? Colonel Stewart-Wilson answered that they did not do that as a fairly firm rule. But he would be rejoining the royal family at Balmoral in mid-September, and he would be happy to take the log with him and ask. Ed thanked him, handed over the log, and asked the colonel if he would sign it, too.

When we went back inside, he took us into a tiny room beside the entrance and asked Ed, Mother, and me to sign the palace guest book, asking Ed, in addition, to indicate beside his signature the way in which he had arrived in Britain. We then returned to our limousine and drove through the gate and across the road, where reporters were waiting to talk to Ed.

That night Ed and I took the tube to Westminster and had a beautiful dinner at St. Stephen's Restaurant. We sat at a corner table looking out at the Houses of Parliament and Big Ben and Westminster Abbey.

The next morning, turned into pumpkins, we returned the suit to Moss Brothers, climbed into our Morris Marina, and set out for the countryside. First stop Stonehenge. Next stop Plymouth and the Mayflower Marina, where we finally met Commander Smith and Mrs. Smith—more new friends—and saw the space reserved for *Folly*. We promised to get her there next year—really.

Also in Plymouth we took care of another bit of unfinished business. The year before, as Ed had set sail on his first attempt to cross the Atlantic, Jake Mottayaw, then mayor of Fernandina Beach, had given him the Key to the City. At the same time he had given Ed a document bestowing the same honor upon the lord mayor of Plymouth. Commander Smith arranged an appointment and accompanied us on this mission. The lord mayor, Mr. Ramsey Thornton, received us graciously in his office.

There was still one more important errand to accomplish in fulfilling all the purposes of Ed's voyage. We couldn't leave England without seeing Malvina and Andy Finlayson and collecting the other half of the dollar bill. Ed had also brought Malvina several cans of sweet potatoes, one of her favorite American foods. Deal, their home, was our last stop before returning to London for our flight home. And between Plymouth and Deal we had seen as much as possible of England, Wales, and Scotland, all the way to Loch Ness. And everywhere the people we met, with their British understanding of the call of the sea, were delighted by Ed's voyage and pleased with his celebration of the Queen's Silver Jubilee. And we learned that there is no English hinterland. Even in what we thought were inland towns, the salt in our blood was comforted by the scream of terns soaring overhead.

On Wednesday, October 19, back at home in Atlanta, Ed received a registered letter from Buckingham Palace. It read:

14th October, 1977

Dear Mr. Lormand,

I was very interested to be able to have a look at the log books which you kept for your voyage across the Atlantic. It must have been a demanding project, but like so many adventures you only really begin to appreciate it when it is all over.

Congratulations on a splendid achievement.

/s/ Yours sincerely,
Philip

The logs were returned shortly afterward, unsigned, as we had expected, but Prince Philip's note was a total surprise and a gesture that we very much appreciated.

Beau Cutts wrote an article in the next morning's *Atlanta Constitution* about Ed's receiving the note. That afternoon we had a call from the British Consulate in Atlanta. Prince Charles was due to arrive for a weekend in Georgia and South Carolina on Friday. The consulate was having a reception for him on Saturday afternoon, and they would be pleased if we could be there.

On the doorstep of Buckingham Palace. Left to right, Ed, holding his logbooks and Govenor Busbee's Proclamation; Eddie Mae Spear, Fran's mother; and Fran, holding the gift for Queen Elizabeth. August 11, 1977. (John Hammond photo)

When I picked up our invitation at the consulate the next morning and also when we arrived at the grounds of Swan House for the reception, we were surprised to find that some effort was being made to see that we were introduced to the prince. We had the feeling that the people at the consulate thought that Prince Charles would be interested in Ed's voyage and that we might provide some relief from the multitudes of businessmen and politicians who had greeted the prince since his arrival.

The reception was held on a beautiful autumn afternoon. The prince arrived on schedule, and we were, indeed, introduced to him. He was apparently both surprised and interested, shook hands with us, and chatted for a few minutes about Ed's trip.

The expected—and sought-after—rewards of Ed's voyage—the reasons why he wanted to go in the first place—were personal and have been personally fulfilling. The many totally unexpected pleasures that have come to both of us as a result of the voyage have included many other people. And in addition to things like getting a note from Prince Philip and meeting Prince Charles, we see the equally exciting response of friends and strangers to the accomplishment of personal adventure as they translate Ed's specific feat into the challenges of their own lives. Not everyone wants to sail the Atlantic singlehanded, but a spirit of adventure is alive and well in the human race.

Navigation Charts and Publications

Chart No. 1, *U.S.A. Nautical Chart Symbols and Abbreviations*
Nautical Almanac (current)
Brown's Nautical Almanac
Reed's Nautical Almanac
Bowditch, *American Practical Navigator*
Mixter, *A Primer of Navigation*
Lane and Montgomery, *Navigation the Easy Way*
Chapman, *Piloting, Seamanship & Small Boat Handling*
H.O. 229, Volumes II, III, and IV, Sight Reduction Tables
Sailing Directions for Bermuda, Azores, South Coast of England, Coasts of France, Portugal, Spain, West Coast of England, Ireland
Coast Pilots for East Coast U.S.
Light Lists and Radio Aids for Europe and East Coast U.S.
Tide Tables for Europe and East Coast U.S.
Small-scale charts of East Coast U.S. to Nova Scotia
Large-scale charts of all major ports East Coast U.S.
Large-scale charts of Bermuda and Azores
Large-scale charts of major ports from Scilly Isles to Portland Bill
Charts of North Atlantic Ocean, Northern and Southern Sheets
Charts of English Channel
Pilot Charts of North Atlantic Ocean, covering all months
Track Chart of the World
Great Circle Sailing Chart of the North Atlantic Ocean (standard and reduced sizes)
Gnomonic Plotting Chart, North Atlantic Ocean
Universal Plotting Sheets
Work Forms (Davis) for H.O. 229 Sight Reduction Tables

Sail Inventory

1976 VOYAGE

Mainsail (two sets reef points)
Working jib
Storm trysail
Storm jib
150% genoa
Spare sail slides, jib hanks, grommets

1977 VOYAGE

Mainsail (two sets reef points), reworked by sailmaker and all sail slides
replaced
Working jib (100% foretriangle), 7.25-oz. material, triple sewn, with one
set reef points to bring it down to storm jib
150% genoa, repaired
130% genoa with one reef to 110%, 7.25-oz. material
Storm trysail
Storm jib
Blue acrylic deck tube for stowing sail on deck
Spare sail slides, jib hanks, grommets, cloth

Medical Supplies

2   rolls 3″ adhesive tape
3   rolls 2″ adhesive tape
2   boxes eye pads
4   Ace bandages (4″ × 2″)
2   dispensers razor blades
2   bottles salt tablets
    Sunscreen: 2 tubes cream, 2 bottles lotion, 3 tubes lip cream
1   triangle bandage
2   packages gauze sponges
2   tubes A & D ointment
20 gauze pads
2   boxes assorted Bandaids
2   pints alcohol
1   box medium butterfly closures
1   box small butterfly closures
2   large bags cotton balls
2   clinical thermometers
1   pair bandage scissors
1   clamp
2   pairs tweezers
1   bottle paregoric
1   bottle Kwell lotion

Air splints (1 arm and 1 leg)
Vaseline
Mercurochrome
Iodine
Hydrogen Peroxide
Merck *Manual*

Dental Kit

Hemostat
Sutures
Disposable syringes with various-sized needles
Reusable syringe
Forceps for pulling teeth
Scalpel
Probe
Dental mirror
Octocaine
Temporary filling
Rubber gloves

Acid Stomach

Mylanta II
Riopan

Chest Pain

Nitroglycerin

Colds and Nasal Congestion

Co-Tylenol Cold Formula
Ru-Tuss

Coughs

Tussend

Constipation

Dialose Plus
Dulcolax suppositories

Cuts

Neosporin antibiotic ointment

Dermatitis, Eczema, Boils

Vioform Hydrocortisone

Diarrhea

Lomotil

Ear Infection
Otobione

Eye Infection
Visine
Neodecadron
Collyrium

Hemorrhoids
Anusol cream

Infection
Ampicillin
Keflex

Itching, Rash, Allergy
Benadryl

Muscle Relaxant (Pulled Muscle)
Parafon Forte

Nausea and Vomiting
Compazine: tablets, injection

Pain
Mild: Aspirin, Tylenol
Moderate: Tylenol #3
Severe: Demerol injections, Demerol tablets

Stomach Cramps
Valpin

Swelling, Puffiness of Extremities
Dyazide

Seasickness
Bucladin

Severe Reaction
Adrenalin

Vitamins
Berocca

Miscellaneous Equipment
and Spares

Engine spares (Universal Atomic 4 kit), 8 quarts oil, pump grease, assorted lubricants, hoses for engine and through-hull fittings, 2 covers for ventilators on stern, 1 plug wrench, 8 extra spark-plugs, 2 sets feeler gauges, 1 hydrometer, 1 copy engine manual
Stove (Optimus) spares: burner, needle valve, pump
Rigging spares: clamps, thimbles, rigging cable
Heavy-duty cable cutters
Sail repair kit: needles, palm, awl, cloth, thread, tape
Bosun's knife
Hull repair kit: underwater putty, fiberglass repair kit, oakum, packing, large assortment of different-sized wooden plugs, assortment of lumber of different sizes and lengths, several yards treated canvas, extra pillows
Spare wicks for lamps and running lights
Electrical: bulbs, electrical wire, fuses, large assortment of spare batteries (radio, RDF, flashlights, tape recorder)
 3 shaft zincs
 6 quarts bottom paint
 3 portable bilge pumps
12 gallons kerosene
15 gallons alcohol
    Heavy-duty boom vang

Rope ladder for climbing mast
2 mechanical alarm clocks
Minute timer
Stopwatch
Chelsea chronometer
Chelsea barometer
Panasonic Tech 1100 receiver
Gladding Gulfstream radio direction finder
2 Panasonic tape recorders
30 hours blank tapes
Hand-held wind speed indicator
Starfinder
One-hand dividers
Large course protractor
Parallel rules
Small course protractor to use with universal plotting sheets
Small calculator
Davis plastic sextant
O.S.K. ¾-size sextant
Walker Rocket taffrail log with spare rotator, 75-foot line, weights
2 pair binoculars
3 compasses: small emergency compass, hand-held Ritchie compass, SN-B-45 Ritchie compass and spare compass light
Avon 4-man life raft with Series "E" survival pack
Emergency locator transmitter
2 radar reflectors
16-gauge pump shotgun: blank shells for percussive effect, bird shot to be used for survival, shells with slugs for repelling sharks
37-mm flare gun with 6 37-mm parachute flares
12 hand-held flares
Hand-held power hailer
Shrimpboat-sized horn (your own lung power)
Red dye marker
Spare netting
1 box stainless steel screws, fittings for self-steerer, cotter pins, etc.
400 feet half-inch line, nylon twist
400 feet eighth-inch line, nylon twist (for lashings, sail ties, emergency replacement of reefing points)
1 large roll shock cord
1 bag industrial-size stainless steel nuts, bolts, and washers (spares for self-steering bracket)

1   set precut, predrilled quarter-inch plywood covers for all portlights with adequate supply of self-tapping stainless steel screws, ready to use

2   galvanized "Kelly" buckets
     White enamel chamber pot

1   set International Signal Code Flags
     Heaving line with lead-loaded monkey's fist
     Lead line for sounding depths

2   spare chimneys for kerosene lamps

3   cigar boxes full of steel nuts, bolts, and washers collected from street gutters over several years of walking

1   cigar box full of extra lighters, pipe cleaners, filters, flints

2   extra logbooks

3   tapes for entertainment; approximately 25 books for entertainment
     Signal mirror
     Bosun's chair
     Extra pair wooden spreaders
     Spare tiller
     Carpenter's hammer
     Ball peen hammer
     Rubber hammer

2   sets flat wrenches
     Small set socket wrenches

2   pipe wrenches (monkey wrench)

2   adjustable wrenches (medium size)

3   pair pliers
     Screwdrivers: 1 large, 3 regular, 1 small; 1 large Phillips, 2 medium Phillips, 1 small Phillips
     Small carpenter's saw with 5 assorted blades
     Coping saw with 6 spare blades

2   hack saws with 12 spare blades
     Metal keyhole saw

1   set wood chisels
     Cold steel chisel
     Steel punch
     Gas blowtorch
     Portable vise
     3-way wood clamp

2   hand drills (mechanical)

2   sets high-speed drill bits

1   set wood drill bits

Hand ratchet screwdriver and drill
Wrecking bar
1   pair vise grip pliers
1   set Allen wrenches
Hobby knife with assorted blades
2   carborundum stones
Wood rasp
2   flat metal files
Rattail metal file
1   pair large metal shears
Hatchet
Machete
2   flexible measuring tapes
1-foot ruler
2   pair goggles
Small wood plane
Steel brush
1   ball steel wool
Assortment of solder
1   can plastic wood
1   container pump grease
1   tube liquid metal
1   can silicone spray
1   can Brasso
1   can penetrating oil
2   cans 3-in-1 oil
1   tube graphite
2   cans epoxy glue
1   tube super glue
2   rolls electrical tape
4   rolls duct tape
Several tubes silicone sealer (clear and white)
Assortment of steel and plastic hose clamps
Large assortment of galvanized nails
Large assortment of brass screws, nuts, bolts
Assortment of sand and emery paper

Food and Galley Items

66 gallons fresh water (including 2 gallons collected
en route as experiment)

Breakfast

 6   single-serving boxes cereal, S*
20   single-serving packs oatmeal, 10 P,* 10 S
20   single-serving packs grits, 10 P, 10 S
12   packs Granola bars, icebox
 6   packs Carnation Instant Breakfast, icebox
 6   cans chocolate Nutrament, 3 P, 3 S
 2   cans vanilla Nutrament, 1 P, 1 S
 6   dozen eggs (1 dozen hardboiled), icebox

Drinks and Juices

 8   six-quart boxes powdered milk, 4 P, 4 S
20   packs ice tea mix, 10 P, 10 S

* P = port lockers; S = starboard lockers

12 packs hot chocolate mix, 6 P, 6 S
3 packs lemonade mix, icebox
2 jars Ovaltine, 1 P, 1 S
1 pack strawberry drink mix, 1 pack grape drink mix, icebox
48 cans (6-oz.) grapefruit juice, 24 P, 24 S
48 cans (6-oz.) pineapple juice, 24 P, 24 S
24 cans V-8, 12 P, 12 S
6 cans apple juice, 3 P, 3 S
Tea bags, S
6 lbs. coffee, 3 P, 3 S

Soups

Cup-a-Soup mixes:
8 chicken noodle, 4 P, 4 S
4 green pea, 2 P, 2 S
8 onion, 4 P, 4 S
8 tomato, 4 P, 4 S
2 cans Chunky Sirloin Burger soup, 1 P, 1 S
2 cans Chunky Beef soup, 1 P, 1 S
2 cans beef with vegetables and barley soup, 1 P, 1 S
2 cans Chunky Vegetable soup, 1 P, 1 S
2 cans bean soup, 1 P, 1 S
2 cans chicken noodle soup, 1 P, 1 S
2 cans tomato soup, 1 P, 1 S

Breads, etc.

1 bag homemade biscuits, icebox
2 1-lb. boxes saltine crackers, 1 icebox, 1 P
1 loaf white bread
4 small loaves French bread, citrus basket
4 lbs. rice in 5 containers, 1 icebox, 1 galley cabinet, 3 S

Meat and Main Dishes

1 can beef chow mein, P
1 can chicken chow mein, S

1   can shrimp chow mein, S
3   cans chow mein noodles, 1 P, 2 S
1   can barbecued pork, S
4   cans tamales, 2 P, 2 S
6   cans chili, 3 P, 3 S
1   can beans and beef, S
2   cans beans and franks (beanie weenies P, chili weenies S)
2   cans pork and beans, 2 S, 1 P
2   cans spaghetti and meat balls, 1 P, 1 S
2   cans beef ravioli, 1 P, 1 S
2   cans macaroni and cheese, 1 P, 1 S
2   cans Salisbury steak with gravy, 1 P, 1 S
2   cans jalapinto beans, 1 P, 1 S
3   cans tuna fish, 2 S, 1 P
4   packs ramen noodles, 2 P, 2 S
1   can roast beef, P
2   cans chicken a la king, 1 P, 1 S
2   small salami sausages, icebox
3   cans spaghetti-o's, 1 P, 2 S
1   can large white lima beans, S
2   packs "Proteinettes" (soy), icebox
5   cans potted meat, 3 S, 2 P
9   cans Vienna sausage, 5 P, 4 S
8   cans sardines, 4 P, 4 S
1   can ham, S
2   jars peanut butter, 1 icebox, 1 liquor cabinet
1   can pork and limas, S
1   can enchiladas and beef, S
3   cans crawfish bisque, S
2   cans shrimp gumbo, S

Vegetables (Canned)

3   cans green beans, 2 S, 1 P
3   cans green peas, 1 S, 2 P
3   cans creamed corn, 1 P, 2 S
1   can whole-kernel corn, S
4   cans asparagus, 2 P, 2 S
2   cans spinach, 1 P, 1 S
1   can sauerkraut, P
3   packs instant mashed potatoes, 1 icebox, 2 P

2   cans white potatoes, 1 P, 1 S
2   cans yams, 1 P, 1 S
2   cans mustard greens, 1 P, 1 S
2   cans turnip greens, 1 P, 1 S
1   can tomatoes, P
2   cans green limas, 1 P, 1 S
1   can beets, P
2   cans okra, 1 P, 1 S
1   can carrots, S
1   can fried rice, P
6   cans sweet potatoes for Malvina

Vegetables (Fresh, Basket on Deck)

2   lbs. onions
2   heads cabbage
2   lbs. carrots
5   lbs. potatoes
1   lb. squash
2   cucumbers

Fruit (Canned)

5   cans peach halves, 3 S, 2 P
4   cans pineapple chunks, 2 S, 2 P
2   cans pears, 1 P, 1 S
4   cans fruit cocktail, 2 P, 2 S
1   can seedless grapes, galley cabinet
1   can applesauce, galley cabinet
2   cans grapefruit sections, 1 P, 1 S
1   can mandarin oranges, galley cabinet

Fruit (Fresh, Citrus Basket, Forward Cabin)

Apples
Bananas
Lemons
Peaches

Grapefruit

1 bag dried mixed fruit, icebox

Sweets

2 jars honey, 1 galley cabinet, 1 P
1 can cane syrup, galley cabinet
1 jar jam, galley cabinet
4 chocolate pudding, 2 P, 2 S
4 butterscotch pudding, 2 P, 2 S
4 banana pudding, 2 P, 2 S
   M&M candies, ice box
1 bag homemade cookies, icebox

Snacks

1 jar popcorn, liquor cabinet
1 lb. process cheese, icebox
1 lb. process cheese with peppers, icebox
1 can mixed nuts, liquor cabinet
2 cans potato sticks, 1 P, 1 S
2 cans fried onions, 1 P, 1 S
1 large can cracklins, S

Wine and Liquor (Liquor Cabinet)

1 bottle Courvoisier
1 bottle ready-mixed martini
1 bottle rum
1 bottle tequila
   Champagne (3 splits, 1 fifth)
1 bottle white wine
1 bottle red wine
2 bottles beer

Staples, Spices, etc.

2 boxes salt, 1 P, 1 S
5 lbs. sugar (2 containers), 1 P, 1 S
5 lbs. plain flour (2 containers), 1 P, 1 S
2 40-oz. boxes Bisquick, 1 P, 1 S
5 lbs. cornmeal (2 containers), 1 P, 1 S
6 packs yeast, galley drawer
1 can Crisco, S
1 jar coarse black pepper, galley cabinet
1 jar red pepper flakes, galley cabinet
   Baking powder, galley cabinet
   Vanilla extract, galley cabinet
   Baking soda, galley cabinet
   Seasoned salt, nutmeg, curry powder, filé powder, chili powder,
     galley cabinet
1 bottle Tabasco, galley cabinet
   Hot pickled pepper sauce, galley cabinet
   Sandwich spread, S

Go-withs (Galley Cabinet)

1 squeeze-jar mustard
1 jar pickle relish
1 jar chutney
1 jar catsup
1 can bell pepper flakes
2 jars olives
1 jar dried onions (chopped)
1 jar dried parsley flakes
1 jar bacon bits
24 chicken bouillon cubes
1 jar margarine

Paper Products, Galley Supplies

2 boxes kitchen matches
2 large cans lighter fluid

20 boxes small matches
 2 packs pipe cleaners
 3 packs filters for cigar holder
    Plastic bags, 2 rolls food-size, 2 boxes sandwich-size
 2 bottles Joy detergent
 4 bars Ivory soap
 1 can nonstick spray for pans
 2 rolls plastic wrap
 4 rolls paper towels
 8 rolls regular toilet paper
 2 boxes Mansize Kleenex
 2 tubes toothpaste
    Toothbrushes
12 boxes cigars
 1 bottle ammonia
 1 bottle Clorox

Bibliography

The following bibliography contains only those books that Ed read during our years of preparation for his voyage (and Fran read most of them at the same time). We began reading about singlehanded and family-crewed voyages and technical information on sailing strategies, boat equipment, and navigation. We soon found ourselves reading maritime history, oceanography, and general survival theory and techniques. Ed reports that he found helpful practical information in every book he read.

As soon as we see this list in print, we are sure we'll remember important books that we should have included, and we know that many fine books that would be helpful in preparing for a singlehanded voyage have been published since 1977. We are still reading and learning. One bit of advice if you are working on a project like this—keep a reading log. It will get very impressive after a while, and if you annotate it, you will be able to find elusive bits of information that you wanted to keep track of.

Allcard, Edward. *Voyage Alone.* New York: Dodd, Mead, 1964.
Alsar, Vital. *La Balsa.* New York: E. P. Dutton, 1973.
Anderson, J. R. L. *The Ulysses Factor.* New York: Harcourt Brace Jovanovich, 1973.
———. *Vinland Voyage.* New York: Funk & Wagnalls, 1967.

Armstrong, Richard. *Themselves Alone.* Boston: Houghton Mifflin, 1972.

Arrow, Neill V. *10,000 Miles to Boston.* New York: Stein & Day, 1964.

Batten, Louis J. *The Nature of Violent Storms.* Garden City, N.Y.: Anchor Books, Doubleday, 1961.

Blyth, Chay. *The Impossible Voyage.* New York: Putnam, 1971.

Bowditch, Nathaniel. *American Practical Navigator.* U. S. Navy Hydrographic Office, 1966.

Caldwell, John. *Desperate Voyage.* Boston: Little, Brown, 1951.

Carlisle, Fred. *Journey with Caravel.* Toronto: Clarke, Irwin, 1971.

Carson, Rachel. *The Sea Around Us.* New York: Oxford University Press, 1950.

Carter, Samuel, III. *The Gulf Stream Story.* Garden City, N.Y.: Doubleday, 1970.

Charlton, Warwick. *The Second Mayflower Adventure.* Boston: Little, Brown, 1957.

Chichester, Sir Francis. *Alone Across the Atlantic.* London: Hodder & Stoughton, 1961.

———. *Gipsy Moth Circles the World.* New York: Coward-McCann, 1968.

———. *The Lonely Sea and the Sky.* New York: Coward-McCann, 1959.

———. *The Romantic Challenge.* New York: Coward, McCann & Geoghegan, 1972.

Chidsey, Donald Barr. *Shackleton's Voyage.* New York: Award Books, 1973.

Coles, K. Adlard. *Heavy Weather Sailing.* Tuckahoe, N.Y.: John de Graff, 1975.

Cook, James. *Captain Cook's Voyages of Discovery.* New York: E. P. Dutton, 1906.

Dana, Richard Henry. *Two Years Before the Mast.* New York: World, 1946.

Davison, Ann. *My Ship Is So Small.* London: Peter Davies, 1956.

Day, John A., and Gilbert L. Sternes. *Climate and Weather.* Reading, Mass.: Addison-Wesley, 1970.

Downs, Hugh. *A Shoal of Stars.* Garden City, N.Y.: Doubleday, 1967.

Dumas, Vito. *Alone Through the Roaring Forties.* Southampton, England: Adlard Coles, 1960.

Freuchen, Peter. *Book of the Seven Seas.* New York: Julian Messner, 1957.

Gerbault, Alain. *The Fight of the Firecrest.* New York: D. Appleton, 1926.

Graham, Robin Lee. *Dove*. New York: Harper & Row, 1972.

Groene, Janet. *Cooking on the Go*. New York: Grosset & Dunlap, 1971.

Hakluyt, Richard. *Voyages & Documents*. London: Oxford University Press, 1958.

Herron, Matt; Jeannine Herron; Matthew Herron; and Melissa Herron. *The Voyage of Aquarius*. New York: E. P. Dutton, 1974.

Heyerdahl, Thor. *Aku-Aku*. Chicago: Rand McNally, 1958.

———. *Kon-Tiki*. Chicago: Rand McNally, 1950.

———. *The RA Expeditions*, Translated by Patricia Crampton. Garden City, N.Y.: Doubleday, 1971.

Hiscock, Eric. *Around the World in Wanderer III*. London: Oxford University Press, 1956.

———. *Beyond the West Horizon*. London: Oxford University Press, 1963.

———. *Cruising Under Sail*. London: Oxford University Press, 1965.

———. *Voyaging Under Sail*. London: Oxford University Press, 1970.

Humble, Richard. *Marco Polo*. New York: G. P. Putnam's Sons, 1975.

Klein, David, and Mary Louise King. *Great Adventures in Small Boats*. London: Collier-Macmillan, 1963.

Knöbl, Kuno, with Arno Dening. *Tai Ki to the Point of No Return*. Boston: Little, Brown, 1975.

Ledyard, John. *John Ledyard's Journal of Captain Cook's Last Voyage*, ed. by James Kenneth Munford. Corvallis, Oreg.: Oregon State University Press, 1963.

Lee, Eric, and Kenneth Lee. *Safety and Survival at Sea*. New York: W. W. Norton, 1972.

Lewis, David. *Ice Bird*. New York: W. W. Norton, 1975.

———. *The Ship Would Not Travel Due West*. New York: St. Martin's Press, 1961.

London, Jack. *Cruise of the Snark*. New York: Macmillan, 1911.

Manry, Robert. *Tinkerbelle*. New York: Harper & Row, 1966.

Marco Polo. *The Travels of Marco Polo*, ed. by Manuel Komroff. New York: Liveright. 1930.

Marin-Marie. *Wind Aloft, Wind Alow*. New York: Scribner's, 1947.

Mattingly, Garrett. *The Armada*. Boston: Houghton Mifflin, 1959.

Melville, Herman. *Moby Dick*.

Moitessier, Bernard. *The Long Way*, translated by William Rodamor. New York: Doubleday, 1970.

Morison, Samuel Eliot. *Admiral of the Ocean Sea*. Boston: Little, Brown, 1942.

———. *Spring Tides*. Boston: Houghton Mifflin, 1965.

Mowat, Farley. *The Boat Who Wouldn't Float*. Boston: Little, Brown, 1969.

Nordhoff, Charles, and James Norman Hall. *The Bounty Trilogy*. Boston: Little, Brown, 1940.

Pidgeon, Harry. *Around the World Singlehanded*. New York: Appleton-Century-Crofts, 1932.

Pigafetta, Antonio. *The Voyage of Magellan, Journal of Antonio Pigafetta*, Translated by Paula Spurlin Paige. Englewood Cliffs, N.J.: Prentice-Hall, 1969.

Read, Piers Paul. *Alive*. Philadelphia: J. B. Lippincott, 1974.

Richards, Joe. *Princess*. New York: David McKay, 1973.

Rickman, John, ed., *Journal of Captain Cook's Last Voyage to the Pacific Ocean*. Ann Arbor, Mich.: University Microfilms, 1966.

Ridgway, John, and Chay Blyth. *A Fighting Chance*. Philadelphia: J. B. Lippincott, 1967.

Robertson, Dougal. *Survive the Savage Sea*. New York: Praeger, 1973.

Robertson, R. B. *Of Whales and Men*. New York: Alfred A. Knopf, 1954.

Robinson, William. *Ten Thousand Leagues Over the Sea*. New York: Harcourt, Brace, 1932.

———. *To the Great Southern Sea*. Tuckahoe, N.Y.: John de Graff, 1956.

———. *A Voyage to the Galapagos*. New York: Harcourt, Brace, 1938.

Rose, Sir Alec. *My Lively Lady*. New York: David McKay, 1969.

Roth, Hal. *Two on a Big Ocean*. New York: Macmillan, 1972.

Shipman, James T.; Jerry L. Adams; Jack Baker; Jerry D. Wilson. *An Introduction to Physical Science*. Lexington, Mass.: D. C. Heath, 1971 (section on weather).

Slocum, Joshua. *Sailing Alone Around the World*. New York: Century, 1900.

———. *Voyage of the Liberdade*. Boston: Roberts Brothers, 1894.

Smeeton, Miles. *Once Is Enough*. New York: W. W. Norton, 1959.

Snow, Edward Rowe. *New England Sea Tragedies*. New York: Dodd, Mead, 1960.

Steele, David J. *Yachtsman in Red China*. Tuckahoe, N.Y.: John de Graff, 1970.

Taberly, Eric. *Lonely Victory*. New York: Clarkson Potter, 1966.

Tazelaar, James, ed. *The Articulate Sailor*. Tuckahoe, N.Y.: John de Graff, 1973.

Teller, Walter Magnes. *The Search for Captain Slocum*. New York: Charles Scribner's Sons, 1956.

Thompson, Thomas. *Lost*. New York: Atheneum, 1975.

Thomson, George Malcolm. *The Search for the Northwest Passage.* New York: Macmillan, 1975.

Tomalin, Nicholas, and Ron Hall. *The Strange Last Voyage of Donald Crowhurst.* New York: Stein & Day, 1970.

Vail, Philip. *The Magnificent Adventures of Henry Hudson,* New York: Dodd, Mead, 1965.

Vihlen, Hugo S. *April Fool.* Chicago: Follett, 1971.

Villiers, Alan. *By Way of Cape Horn.* New York: Charles Scribner's Sons, 1953.

———. *The Cruise of the Conrad.* New York: Charles Scribner's Sons, 1937.

———. *The Grain Race.* New York: Charles Scribner's Sons, 1933.

———. *Wild Ocean.* New York: McGraw-Hill, 1957.

Walker, Nicolette Milnes. *When I Put Out to Sea.* New York: Stein & Day, 1972.

Wibberley, Leonard. *Toward a Distant Island.* New York: Ives-Washburn, 1969.

Williams, Geoffrey. *Sir Thomas Lipton Wins.* Philadelphia: J. B. Lippincott, 1970.

Williams, Harold, ed. *One Whaling Family.* Boston: Houghton Mifflin, 1964.

Willis, William. *The Gods Were Kind.* New York: E. P. Dutton, 1955.

Winston, Alexander. *No Man Knows My Grave.* Boston: Houghton Mifflin, 1969.

Wynne, Barry. *The Man Who Refused To Die.* New York: Paperback Library, 1967.

Periodicals

Yachting since 1964.
Sail since 1971.
Motor Boating & Sailing since 1972.